Taxi, Limousine, and Transport Network Company Regulation

The vehicle for hire (VFH) market – broadly comprising taxis, limousines, and app-based transport – has faced multiple and significant changes over the years, with the period since 2010 a time of major upheaval. This book documents the development of the market over time, examining its regulation and control structures, exploring its history, trends, and market theories, and discussing how these are both promoted and challenged by the changes affecting the sector.

This book reviews recent developments in the VFH industry, from the influx of new market entrants and the emergence of app-based services to their widespread use, comparing international markets and their regulation, and draws on a series of case studies in key locations in North America, Europe, and Asia. It establishes and details economic, market, social, and political theory affecting the VFH industry and devotes its second half to the definition and emergence of transport typologies and markets in which the sector has a role (or potential role). The book concludes, from a neutral standpoint, on the balance between market participants, addressing the immediate future facing the industry, including the impacts of Covid and other external factors. It considers the short- and long-term effects of market change, the role played by regulators, and the market conditions imposed upon them.

Written for industry practitioners – both suppliers and regulators – as well as the academic community, this book will inform the community and prompt further analysis of a significant and growing field in transportation.

Dr. James M. Cooper is Director at Transport Research Partners and Project Manager for the Tayside and Central Scotland Regional Transport Partnership (Tactran), UK.

Jørgen Aarhaug is Senior Research Economist at the Institute of Transport Economics (TØI), Oslo, Norway.

John Scott is Operations Director (retired) in the Department of For Hire Vehicles, Government of the District of Columbia.

Wim Faber is Managing Director of Challans and Faber.

Taxi, Limousine, and Transport Network Company Regulation
Recurring Challenges

James M Cooper, Jørgen Aarhaug,
John Scott, and Wim Faber

Routledge
Taylor & Francis Group

LONDON AND NEW YORK

Designed cover image: www.123rf.com – Peshkova

First published 2023
by Routledge
4 Park Square, Milton Park, Abingdon, Oxon OX14 4RN

and by Routledge
605 Third Avenue, New York, NY 10158

Routledge is an imprint of the Taylor & Francis Group, an informa business

British Library Cataloguing-in-Publication Data
A catalogue record for this book is available from the British Library

ISBN: 9781032188034 (hbk)
ISBN: 9781032187655 (pbk)
ISBN: 9781003256311 (ebk)

DOI: 10.4324/9781003256311

Typeset in Bembo
by codeMantra

To Tom, Jaime, and Katie, we dedicate this to you and recognise your role.

Contents

Acknowledgements

To our unsung, hidden but essential friends. You pushed, persuaded, coerced, and co-authored this book, thank you.

Introduction

In any large city, at the corner of downtown blocks, sitting at a taxi stand outside mainline railway terminals, or just beyond the exit doors at airports, you are likely to find a taxi – a small(ish) licensed vehicle available on demand for the transport of individuals and small groups of passengers to destinations requested at the point of use. Similarly, many towns and cities have, on request, a pre-booked service of the same or similar vehicles dispatched at the request of, and to a pick-up point defined by, the intending passenger. The concept being so universal that its presence in a transport hierarchy appeared self-evident, rarely talked about, and relatively uncontroversial. The term 'taxi' is also used widely as a descriptor for many such services, as a verb 'to taxi …home', alongside its more formal legal description as a 'Hackney Carriage' in parts of the UK, and sometimes 'cab' more frequently used in the USA than Europe.

That is until recently. Not that the taxi industry, or trade (as it can portray itself), has been without change, nor, indeed, without controversy, but on few occasions has the industry faced upheaval on the scale experienced in its current iteration. The current market upheaval has resulted from the emergence of smartphone application (app)-based 'taxi' services, including but not limited to UberCab, launched in 2009 (later rebranded as Uber Technologies Inc.), and Lyft Inc. (formerly Zimride), both large US-based corporations dominating the American market; Didi (Didi Chuxing Technology Co.) of China; Grab, Ola, and others in more focused/regional markets. The (sub) sector is frequently referred to by its brand names, such as 'Uber' and 'Lyft',[1] rather than a generic title, such as transportation network companies (TNC), to a far greater extent than seen in the traditional 'taxi' market. The TNC company is associated almost exclusively with smartphone applications (apps), originally used to dispatch private hire vehicles (PHVs),[2] within the for hire vehicle (FHV) market.[3]

As smartphone technologies developed, so too the functionality of the app. Significant additions, to the app, include the use of a person-oriented and highly accurate location beacons permitting rapid identification of locations. This is joined in recent history by artificial intelligence (AI) algorithms that have changed the face of the taxi market and that of personal transportation

DOI: 10.4324/9781003256311-1

in its wider sense. Also, highly significant is the approaches of the app companies themselves, as highly motivated and visibly aggressive proponents of their technologies, operating both at a far larger geographical scale than their taxi predecessors and a significantly more targeted/politically astute lobby than seen before.

The subsequent period, from around 2010 to date, has seen the development of app-based services growing rapidly, responding to the outward visibility of its proponents, and the oft-claimed fact that the app allowed a service that was, by default, better than its traditional taxi rivals. Customers, after selecting the app, quickly became used to fast pick-up and delivery, together with frequently lower fares,[4] which were made possible by the contractual and service relationships established between the app companies and their drivers. The second and subsequent generations of the more popular apps moved away from a Limousine-oriented service[5] to a private non-professional driver,[6] with many of the more recent start-ups concentrating exclusively on this supply model.

The move to a non-professional driver market appears to have supported both fare reductions and vehicle availability characteristics that allowed TNCs to compete directly with the market segment previously dominated by taxis. Indeed, the lack of formal qualification and/or the reduced regulatory burden of the TNCs, it is argued, place the app company at a market advantage, creating a new segment under the banners of Lyft, UberX, and UberPop,[7] amongst others. The segment lacks a formal global definition/term but is frequently referred to as TNCs – a common but not universal term applied in North America, while members of the public appeared to prefer to use the companies brand name, and the companies themselves 'ride-sharing', despite the latter term having a pre-existing use and differing meanings.

Initially, the combination of new technology and a new modus operandi meant that the taxi and FHV industry were caught on the back foot. In many locations, and maybe as a sop to maintain distinctions between taxis and TNCs, the traditional taxi industry was granted exclusive access to the hail or taxi stand markets, though this too would decline as the market moved toward a new equilibrium. The cruising market, one of the market segments initially reserved for traditional taxis, was later joined by 'eHailing', the extension of apps to the cruising market. The term 'eHail' emerging from New York, USA, based on the observed practice where app-based vehicles would be 'hailed' electronically, and thus entering the 'exclusive' market previously afforded to taxis alone. The concept of e-hailing may be superfluous, however, as the underlying use of the app for 'asap transport' fulfils many of the underlying demands for immediate transport on demand, cruising while waiting app dispatched trips already being common amongst TNC drivers; while it is also observed that TNC dispatch may already have resulted in more rapid pick-ups than the traditional seek and hail activities reserved for taxis alone. It is also noticeable, over the earlier parts of the rebalancing period, that various forms of contract work also remained aligned to the taxi, mainly in the non-emergency medical transport (NEMT) and social and education transport sectors, though later market shifts moved, perhaps inevitably, to a TNC role in this too.

The most recent chapter, recovery from the Covid pandemic, is also of significance and reveals yet another twist in market development that may, at first, appear counterintuitive. As many countries lessened restrictions on movement first set up to slow Covid, including those on travel and international arrivals, a possibly predictable rush to travel occurred. Tourism has, at the time of writing, re-emerged, with previously suppressed demand translating to a rush to get away. Work trips to traditional workplaces have also restarted, albeit without the pent-up demand, aka: peaking, visible in the leisure market. The extent to which work-based travel will regain pre-pandemic levels has, at the time of writing, yet to be seen, with many industries returning to work using hybrid models of attendance. The subsequent 'post-Covid' increase in demand for travel, including demand for taxis, has come face to face with a depleted level of supply, as drivers have left the industry, a direct result of a lack of demand during the pandemic. In short, the industry faces a sudden and significant lack of supply. The twist emerges in the approach of both taxis and TNCs to the shortage, with an unexpected, though ultimately logical, thawing of relations between the two sides. In short, TNCs and taxis appear to be willing to work with each other in meeting the increased demand. TNCs sign arrangements with taxi companies, more precisely with taxi app competitors, to add the taxi fleet as suppliers to their apps, while for the taxi side the arrangement appears to, have the potential to, stem a loss of business to the TNCs. In short, a short-term win-win. The extent to which such entente cordiale remains, well – cordial, is yet to be seen. Previous excursions into TNCs dispatching taxis appear to have worked poorly but remain to be seen in the instance of the current iteration.

This book takes a detailed photo of the last two decades and delves deeply in the start, the growth and development of the ride-sharing companies, and the way they influenced rulemaking and control and changed the landscape for the taxi and FHV industry. A period in which both the taxi and FHV industry changed, and the app sector evolved. It was a more profound change than the last technological development which shook and reshaped both industries: the rise of radio and (following on from that) electronic dispatching.

Notes

1 The term 'Uber' is a trade name owned and applied by Uber Technologies Inc. to a wide cross-section of its services. The term is also observed in use as a more generic title for transportation network companies (TNCs), e.g.: 'to Uber... home'. Alternatives based on other brands also apply, including 'Lyft' in North America.
2 Includes 'Black Car' Services, Limousines (Limos), Private Hire Cars, and Minicabs amongst others.
3 AKA: the (generic) 'Taxi' market.

4 TNC fares can vary, including variations on the basis of observed demand patterns under a form of multiplier referred to as 'surge pricing' in some reports. As a result, the fare paid is not always lower than taxi rates.

5 The term Limousine (Limo) is applied across a large number of North American locations to relate to professional for hire services also bearing the terms Town Car and Black Car in some US cities. The term is distinct from Luxury Limousines (stretch limousines), though these may be provided by the same companies in some instances. Some equivalences exist in Europe, including private hire vehicles/PHCs in the UK.

6 The term 'non-professional driver' is used here to denote drivers who may not have completed driving tests, obtained qualifications, or held additional licences, beyond those required for a car driver in general.

7 UberPop is a brand applied in a number of European countries, which is broadly equivalent to the UberX service in North America, though some regulatory and licensing differences do exist. The distinction is neither universal nor country based, with UberX also appearing in European countries. Common branding applied between countries, e.g.: UberX in both the USA and the UK, does not equate identical licensing.

1 Defining the Taxi and For Hire Industry

Taxis, limousines, and private hire vehicles (PHVs), collectively the for hire vehicle (FHV) industry, have a long-standing role in the provision of transport in most cities and the vast majority of countries around the world. The FHV market has emerged over decades and centuries, initially focused on the taxicab, and its forerunner, the 'Hackney'; to be joined by an additional tier of PHVs in the mid to late 20th century,[1] and by app-based[2] 'taxi-like' services, commonly known as transportation network companies (TNCs) in the USA,[3] widely visible in the period since 2010. Both traditional taxis and more recent market entrants provide transport on demand for individuals and small groups between locations defined at, or close to, the time of travel or booking.

The term 'taxi' appears as associated with the vehicle type and the concept of immediate or 'on-demand' transport from around 1897, though the concept existed prior to this point, and has since become a common term used to describe the vehicle, its licence, and use. The term 'taxi' appears virtually unchanged in a surprisingly large number of languages, while others use homophones creating a series of novel and interesting spellings of a word with the same meaning and pronunciation worldwide. More recent trends to adopt terms associated with App-based service providers (TNCs), which mirror many of the facets of the taxi, appear more concentrated on the corporate brands rather than broader industry terms, an aspect that may exacerbate perceived differences between the service types.

The generic term 'taxi' can also be used to cover the wider range of vehicle types, collectively FHVs,[4] including PHVs,[5] limousines, and TNCs, though these will often operate under divergent or differing controls (see Table 1.1). The collective terms, FHV and 'taxi', in their broader sense, may also be used to incorporate other variations on the same theme, including minicabs, jitneys, and similar vehicle types, discussed below, most sharing the characteristics of a small vehicle available for hire with driver for individual or small group use. These gave rise to the concepts of 'on-demand' transport, demand responsive transport (DRT), and flexible transport (FT), though the latter, DRT and FT, can also refer to other forms of transport discussed as a part of the public transport (PT) (*US: Transit*) market, in and of itself demonstrating the (potential for) intersection between FHV and PT modes. Table 1.1

DOI: 10.4324/9781003256311-2

Table 1.1 Taxonomy of names and terms applied to describe for hire vehicles

Descriptive terms applied to vehicle type categorisation

	Terms common in North American English	Terms common in European English	Localised specific variations of English terms
Vehicle available for hire and reward, for engagement on street. **Cruising/hail** Can also include vehicles engaged at a taxi stand/rank. **Stand/ranking taxis**	**Taxi** {USA/Canada/Mex} (Cruising Taxi)	**Hackney Carriage** {GB} Public Hire Taxi {NI} (Hackney/ Hack) (Street Taxi) (Black Taxi – Not NI)	**Small Public Service Vehicle** {IRL}
Vehicle available for hire and reward by pre-booking. **Pre-booked/ dispatched**	**Limousine** {USA/ Canada/Mex} (Livery Vehicle) (Dispatch Vehicle) (Car Service) (Black Car)	**Private Hire Vehicle** {England and Wales, not London} **Private Hire Car** {Scotland} **Private Hire Taxi** {NI} **Minicab** {London} (Taxicab)	**Hackney** {IRL}
Vehicle available for hire and reward by pre-booking via an online platform. **Transportation network company (TNC)**	**Transportation Network Company** {many US and Canadian locations} (Private Transportation Company) (Transportation Network Providers) Frequent use of trade name or corporate ID	None specific Frequent use of trade name or corporate ID Can be incorporated into existing categories, such as Pre-booked {UK} and {IRL}	
Vehicle available for hire and reward, by hailing or pre-booking, when operating a defined route or line as a vehicle in multiple shared occupancy. **Taxibus**	**Jitney** Transportation Network Company, operating in one of line, pool, or similar shared use modes (Dollar Van) (Gypsy Cab) (Neighbourhood Van)	**Taxibus** (Community Transport) (Demand Responsive Transport)	**Public Light Bus** {HK} **Micro/ Minibus/ Kombis** {Egypt/South Africa}

Entries in bold denote a legal definition. Capitalised names are adopted as a primary term describing the segment in this book.

illustrates the terminology commonly applied to the mode, including regional variations. Figure 1.1 illustrates the relationship between spontaneous and planned use by regulatory category. Distinctions between booking for single and multiple trips may also affect the choice of vehicle and categories best suited to provide services, as illustrated in Figure 1.2.

Variations in terminology are not uncommon, with many reflecting a localised use or regional dialectal adaptation. Thus, the term private hire 'car', rather than private hire 'vehicle', is more common in Scotland compared to other parts of the UK. Similarly, the term 'chara', itself a derivative of 'charabanc', can be used in Merseyside to relate to bus types of use, whether

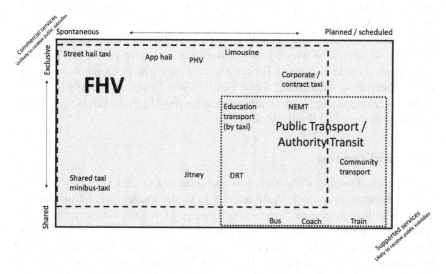

Figure 1.1 Vehicle by regulatory category mapped against use characteristics.
Source: Authors.

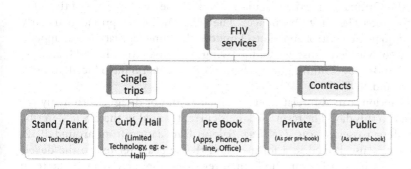

Figure 1.2 Trip type engagement methods and technologies.
Source: Authors.

as a term for all buses, or specific uses, such as smaller taxibus or stage bus operations. In Ireland, the term 'Hackney' is applied to PHVs, putting its use in conflict with those applied elsewhere in Europe, where hackney carriage can be a legal term for taxis, rather than private hire. In Northern Ireland, the term taxi is more often applied to PHVs, *NI Eng: Private Hire Taxi*, insofar as the majority of the Northern Ireland market is served by PHVs. Additional geographical terms are applied to Belfast, as distinct from the rest of Northern Ireland. Taxis available for street hailing in Northern Ireland (*Scot Eng: Hackney Carriages*) are distinguished by the addition of public hire to the description, *NI Eng: Public Hire Taxis*. Local language variations also exist in other countries, the Irish language 'Tacsi', pronounced as per the anglicised 'Taxi', legally defined in Ireland as a small public service vehicle (SPSV), while some languages differ between singular and plural, as in German 'Taxe' (singular) and 'Taxen' (plural). Taxibus services can also follow a variety of names, of which jitney is the most common in the USA. Other derivatives include dolmus in Turkey and taxi collectifs in francophone countries. Alternative originating terms can be more linked to bus types: public light bus (Hong Kong) and variants of micro-bus (Egypt), minibus, or kombis (combinations) in South Africa.

Historical Origins

The historical nature of the market is also reflected in its definitions, etymology, and forms of control. Early references to the mode appear from around 1610, including in France: 'Voitures de Louage' (*UK Eng: Vehicles for Hire*) and 'Hackney Carriages (Hackney Cabs)', in the UK, from around the same time. Variations in vehicle types include the 'Chaise a Bras', a Sedan Chair carried by human 'bearers', patented in France in 1617, and licensed as a vehicle for hire; the same vehicle was introduced in the UK around 1634.

Horse-drawn 'Growlers' were four-wheeled hackney carriages named after the growling noise reported as the vehicle crossed cobbled streets. Growlers are documented in the UK from around 1654, with regulations applied under the Ordinance for the Regulation of Hackney Coachmen[6] of the same year (the 1654 Hackney Ordinance). The 1654 Ordinance provided an early form of quantity control applied to London; the same legislation was applied to the two-wheeled hansom cab, following its introduction in 1834, and the motorised Bersley hummingbird, a battery-powered taxi introduced, in London, around 1897.

Descriptions can also relate to the vehicle layout or design, with many remaining to this day. The term 'Sedan' is currently used in the US to describe a four-door passenger car, *UK Eng*: Saloon Car, dating from around 1912. The term is also linked to a form of taxi that appears related to the development of Chaise a Bras in the French region of the same name. The term 'van' is also seen in North America to describe a 'minivan', being a vehicle typically with a higher roofline creating more headroom for a passenger,[7] and in some instances, sufficient in-vehicle space for carriage of a passenger in a wheelchair. Wheelchair accessibility gave rise to the term wheelchair accessible vehicle (WAV),[8] and a subset of vehicle designs specific to that purpose, whether as converted 'vans' or purpose-built for the market segment.

Taxi 'derivatives', often based around specific uses, are also visible in the historical context. The concept of a taxibus arose around 1915 in Southern California, under the term 'Jitney'. Taxibuses allow the carriage of multiple distinctly separate passengers in the same vehicle at the same time. Fares would be charged separately for each passenger, originally at 5¢ per ride, giving rise to the term 'Jitney', the localised slang term for a nickel (*5¢ US coin*).

Jitney services became popular following the Great Depression, and has continued through a number of initiatives, sometimes associated with unlicensed operations to date. The taxibus was most commonly visible where other forms of public transport were absent. Examples include South African townships (jitneys); US cities (jitneys, gypsy taxi) serving areas of social deprivation; and Northern Ireland (Black Taxis [shared]) serving communities with a historically limited public transport service.

A direct link can be drawn from the early emergence of the mode to the current structure and regulations applied to the industry. The term 'hackney carriage' remains in UK legislation,[9] while the basic tenets of quantity

Image 1.1 Two generations of wheelchair accessible London taxi side by side.
Source: Authors.

Image 1.2 Informal public transport: jitneys and taxibuses.
Source: Authors.

and quality controls also remain. Technological innovation is also significant in that a majority of step changes in the taxi industry, whether in terms of patterns of use, regulation, or vehicle design, can be traced to specific innovations or social events discussed below. Major events include, but are not limited to, the introduction of new vehicle technologies, industrial disputes, and/or changes in market conditions. These can appear revolutionary, often associated with step changes, not least, as examples, the introduction of motorised vehicles and the recent development of apps, though more subtle evolutionary changes are also visible and discussed below.

Social Drivers of Change

Social issues affecting the taxi industry have played a significant role in the development of the market and the regulations that control it. These include periods of aggressive and destructive competition, recorded as 'taxi wars' in some reports, often associated with periods of societal change and economic turbulence, such as the Great Depression of the 1920s.

In most instances, 'taxi wars' appear as aggressive rivalries. They can include a range of underhand or anticompetitive tactics deployed by some, seeking to gain market share by undermining the operations of a rival, while others appear more severe. The South African market provides an example of rivalries leading to violence, including reported turf-wars, gang-war, and mafia-like tactics, many reported in recent history and worsening in the period since 1987, which may also be linked to policies of taxi deregulation in the country, discussed below.

Hostile rivalries are not specifically new events, with clashes documented back to the earliest reports of the mode itself. In London, around 1623, the Thames Watermen were reported as calling for hackney coaches to be '*suppressed*', likely to equate to a (desired) ban on taxis, or their severe limitation. The call did not, of itself, appear sufficient to prevent the development of the taxi market, resulting in a short-lived and abortive form of quantity control. In 1634, the introduction of a taxi rank, at the Maypole in The Strand, provided an early example of the market for taxi engagement,[10] at the same time demonstrating that the earlier calls for suppression had been largely unsuccessful. The Maypole rank was reported as provided for the exclusive use of Bailey's vehicles, a large operator of hackney carriages at the time, with other taxi competitors to follow with their own ranks in due course.

Competitive ranks followed from other operators around the same time, most focusing on The Strand as a central London location. The agglomeration of multiple ranks over a small area created a sufficient amount of negative publicity as to warrant a Royal Proclamation, by King Charles 1st, on 19 January 1635, to '*restrain the multitude and promiscuous use of coaches about London and Westminster and expressly command and forbid that no hackney coaches or hired carriages be used or suffered in London, Westminster or suburbs thereof except they be to travel at least 3 miles out of the same*'.

While it is reported that the 1635 proclamation had only limited effect in the supply and race to supply between taxi companies, the competitive nature of the industry appears to have created the conditions for the 1654 Hackney Ordinance. The 1654 act limited the number of 'hackney coaches' in London and Westminster to 300, thereby creating the first successful example of quantity control in the London market.

The use of hackney carriages appears to have grown in the period from 1654, though growth was limited at various points of social upheaval, including the outbreak of the Great Plague of London in 1665. Further regulations are reported from 1661, including the concept of licence fees, one of the first recorded instances of economic regulation in the city, and the appointment of William Congreve as commissioner for the licensing of hackney carriages in 1694. Further regulations followed including in 1711, updating economic regulations that developed both licence and distance-based taxation, and, in 1768, the distinction between stand and hailed markets, permitting fewer vehicles to ply for hire than were permitted to stand at taxi ranks.

By the late 1820s, the market had bifurcated, with the introduction of line-based bus services, defined as omnibuses at the time. Significant similarities existed between the two service types, bus and taxi, with the earliest omnibus routes picking up and dropping off on demand at any point, distinct from the hackney carriage by adherence to a route (line), though the choice of route appeared within the control of the operator, without a need for notice of change. Omnibus (bus) services appeared in the UK around 1824 in Manchester, 1829 in London, in France from 1826 in Nantes and 1828 in Paris, and from 1825 in Berlin. The nascent bus industry faced many of the same issues as experienced in the taxi industry, including destructive competition, and resulted in similar regulatory responses, including the 1832 Stagecoach Act, which permitted (formalised) bus behaviours to take up and set down passengers in the streets in London. Rivalries between bus operators also followed, including reported races between bus companies and competition between bus and taxi sectors. In many instances, the result of 'taxi wars' has been the development of regulation – seeking to reduce or avoid the causes of the conflict. Early regulations include quantity controls, a process of regulation that remains to this day.

External factors are also visible, including the Great Depression, a worldwide economic decline reported in the USA from 1929;[11] the depression created a surplus of supply, as large numbers of recently unemployed people sought work in the taxi industry, leading to unsustainable/destructive competition in the market. The depression created similar circumstances as reported in the UK some hundred years prior and resulted in the introduction of quantity and quality controls applied to the American taxi market in an attempt to stabilise and regulate competition (Gilbert and Samuels, 1982; Davis, 1998). It is important to note that regulation applied in the light of each change appears to be focused on regulating, rather than eliminating, competition, being an important distinction that remains significant to this day.

The current market for taxi services can also be affected by parallel social and economic factors, including those emerging as a result of the Covid-19 pandemic, which have affected demand for transport. Crossover impacts are also visible, between technological development and societal expectations. Current shifts in the market include proactive responses to booking technologies as well as a shift in regulatory approaches from regulated competition to a focus on anti-trust enforcement (OECD, 2018).

Technical Drivers of Change

Technical drivers of change exist alongside, and in some instances, as a facet of social change. Historically, the taxi industry, where recognised as a single form of transport, has experienced advances in vehicle design, motive power, measurement technologies, and methods of engagement. Each aspect provides both opportunity to the sector and challenges to its control.

Human-powered traction (Chaises a Bras) was rapidly overtaken by horse-drawn vehicles, with a period of around two centuries in which carriage designs were updated and replaced in an effort to provide passenger comfort as a competitive advantage. Carts were replaced by carriages and coaches, including market splits to distinguish between line (bus) and passenger-defined route (hackney/taxi) options. In 1834, a patent design was registered for the hansom cab, and an improved hansom cab was patented by Chapman and Gillet in 1836. The hansom cab providing an enclosed passenger space separated from the driver, reported as a significant improvement on the growler carriages that preceded it.

In the 1890s, the first motorised vehicles appeared. Amongst the first 'horseless' cabs, the battery-powered 'Bersey' was brought into service in London by the London Electrical Cab Company in 1897, quickly earning the nickname of 'Hummingbird', a reference to the sound made during operation. The Bersey was operated on battery power, with a reported range of 30 miles between charges, highlighting a continuing conflict between range and demand. The Bersey was reported as having suffered from poor reliability and was quickly followed by internal combustion engine vehicles, including the Prunel taxi (1903, Paris). By 1906, taxi design elements were also brought under regulatory control, with the introduction of Metropolitan Conditions of Fitness (MCF) to the London market, a measure defining required operating parameters of the emerging vehicle type. The application of MCF requirements to the London fleet was quickly followed by the adoption of similar controls in other UK cities, often based on carbon-copied regulation, though this has not been without controversy as the MCF provides, and continues to apply, (stringent) *de facto* limits to the types of vehicles that may be used as taxis, with the result that few manufacturers seek to provide compliant vehicle designs. Early examples of compliant vehicles include the distinct 'London Taxi' design, originally introduced in 1948 with the Austin Carbodies London Taxi; while many of the subsequent compliant vehicle types bear distinct echoes of the 1948 original.

Communications and Measurement

Two further technological innovations are significant to the current market: the development of the taximeter, a method of recording and measuring tariff; and improving information and communications technologies (ICTs). While separate in their development, and in many aspects of application, both communications and the measurement of fares have been connected in recent market change, including arguments concentrated on the nature and regulation of the industry, discussed below.

The current concept of a measured fare, fares measured against use, originated with the development of the taximeter (*German: Taxemeter*), invented in Germany in 1891 based on a mechanical system to measure charges amongst vehicles for hire. The taximeter was a significant step in the development of fare regulation and has been widely adopted. The term 'Taxi' was derived from the anglicised version of 'Taxe' (*German: meaning tax or fee*), being more readily applied than 'hackney carriage/cab', the most common English term in widespread use prior to this date.

Prior to the development of the taximeter, fares had been typically determined through the use of stated route origins and destinations, often as published tables, with a regulated requirement for the display of fares on the exterior panels of the vehicle and coach bodies in some locations. Origin/destination fare tables have been largely superseded by the use of a taximeter and tariff, while the requirement to display information on fare to passenger

Image 1.3 Early generations of mechanical taximeters.
Source: Authors.

remains in many locations.[12] The nature of the taximeter is also not without significance and is itself subject to a series of controls. The significance arises from the concept of regulatory assurance, the role of a regulator in maintaining balance within the market, itself a form of ensuring fair regulated competition, as opposed to open or free competition. The meter is an active element in measuring regulated fares (economic regulation) and thus falls under 'Specifications, Tolerances, and Technical Requirements for Weighing and Measuring Devices' in a large number of locations in the USA,[13] and it is subject to similar regulation, inspection, and 'sealing'[14] in the UK[15] and elsewhere.

More recent market entrants, including PHVs and TNCs, have argued against the use of taximeters, equating the use of their own app-based measurement as an equivalent to the taximeter, though a majority of jurisdictions continue to require the use of a hard-wired (traditional) meter in their taxi markets, and in many instances, in parallel PHV markets.

TNCs have been more successful in moving away from taximeter use than incumbent PHVs, arguing that the app itself fulfils the role of the taximeter, with most of the larger app companies avoiding the need to comply with regulated tariffs in most locations. While many of the same principles of time and distance measurements apply, TNC measurement is based on GPS positioning rather than a vehicle-connected or mechanical measure of distance.

ICT equipment and functionality are also pivotal to the current market development. App engagement provides a contrast to other forms of engagement which is often dependent on a physical presence/proximity, either where an empty vehicle could be hailed by an intending passenger ('plying for hire')[16] or engaged at a taxi rank. The rank (stand)[17] being a defined lo-cation for taxis to stand, where an intending passenger may be able to engage a vehicle with a greater degree of certainty than street hailing alone. While both hailed and rank markets remain in widespread use to this day, a third market, based on vehicle dispatch/pre-booking, has emerged.

The dispatch market is focused on vehicles attending a 'pick-up' point specified at the time of booking and has been significantly boosted by the emergence of ICTs. Technological development includes the emergence of two-way radios, introduced from the early 1940s (Vrkic, 2017), the more recent development of Internet/web bookings, and the current development of smartphone apps. The latter, the app, offers significant additional benefits of geographical precision for both passenger and driver and automates many of the engagement processes previously undertaken in a dispatch office. The increased accuracy and levels of automation reduce the need to provide a lo-cally based dispatch office, allowing for the merging of dispatch into regional or national activities, including a centralisation of YellowCab dispatch in the USA and cloud-based dispatch functions applied by many TNCs and some taxi companies. It is notable that centralised, regional, or national dispatch may go against local Licensing regulations that may require a city-based or local presence, leading to differences in interpretations in some instances.

Regulatory Definitions

Consistent throughout the development of the taxi has been the presence of a relationship between the mode and the authorities/administrations in whose areas the services operate. The role of the authority often is that of a regu-lator, applying controls (regulations) to the FHV services in their area, with many of the areas of regulation common between locations. Individual reg-ulations can often be traced to specific events that have impacted negatively on the public, creating the circumstances under which a regulation may be seen as beneficial, while a number of regulatory actions can also result from external pressures, including political and economic priorities, and, in some instances, company lobbying.

Early forms of regulation include quantity controls, which may be linked to market oversupply. One of the first examples is the 1654 Hackney Ordi-nance in the UK, which was introduced to limit the number of vehicles operating at any one time, protecting the public from 'destructive competi-tion'. Similar regulations have become commonplace in many jurisdictions, and are sometimes referred to as 'Taxi Caps', or quantity regulation. Other regulations are also observed to follow from specific 'protections' that in-clude, but are not limited to, the development of economic controls affecting the collection of taxation by a government department, the rate of fares per-missible, and/or market controls applied to lease rates within the industry; and safety and quality controls, as may relate to the vehicle and/or driver. The resulting range of regulations can be attributed to the quantity, quality, and economic (QQE) constraints applied to the industry. All areas of the taxi industry are subject to some forms of regulatory control, though the extent of regulation and the regulatory bodies responsible may vary by location and service type.

It is also apparent that differing views of regulation, its significance and application, exist within the industry, between the industry and its regulators, and on a more philosophical basis, whether regulation is desirable or appropriate. It is also observable that the different market segments within the taxi market can be subject to different regulations even when administered by the same authority. Thus, the traditional taxi (hackney carriage) is likely to be more heavily regulated than either the PHV or TNC. It is also important to note, however, that even where regulations have been applied 'lightly',[18] there appears to be a common acceptance of minimum standards of driver and vehicle safety by most suppliers in most locations.

Vehicle Definitions

While it is possible to use the term 'taxi' in a generic sense, applied across regulatory boundaries or as a verb to describe the action of taking a vehicle for hire, such uses can restrict the discussions to the general rather than the specific. Indeed, the emergence of newer operating patterns, such as those used by app companies, supports the need to develop a more specific set of definitions. To do so, we distinguish between the vehicle operating characteristics and the set of regulations under which they operate (see Table 1.1).

In addition to the three primary FHV forms, taxis, PHV, and TNC, a further two categories are sometimes associated with the mode. These are taxibuses,[19] a crossover category where a taxi vehicle is used to provide a bus-like service/operating pattern, and luxury limousines (and other specialist vehicles, including party vehicles).[20]

The taxibus is of specific interest in the current review of regulatory change, as it represents a cross-over between taxi and public transport operation; current examples of which include Belfast Black Taxis, Washington DC Neighborhood Ride, and Uber Transit, amongst others. The operating model of a taxibus/jitney[21] is relatively simple but not as precisely defined as that of the traditional taxi, often as a result of its operating at the edges of the regulations defined for the taxi. A taxibus adopts many of the aspects of a traditional route or line-based bus operation, though the extent to which the taxibus mirrors a traditional bus will vary by location. Consistent aspects are likely to include the carriage of multiple independent passengers and may include the charging of separate fares by passenger and the (dynamic) adaptation of pick up and drop off points (PUDOs) to meet the chosen origins/destinations of multiple passengers. The taxibus concept has moved in and out of fashion at various points in time and can be allied to failures in other modes in some locations, with specific examples including North and West Belfast Black Taxis, the Soweto Taxibus, and the Pittsburgh Hill District, providing mass transit in locations and at times of a significant lack of traditional bus

Image 1.4 Washington DC Taxis at stand, displaying uniform taxi color-scheme.
Source: Authors.

Image 1.5 Unmarked TNC vehicle, in Amsterdam, displaying TNC plates.
Source: Authors.

Image 1.6 Stretched limousine operating as a luxury vehicle.
Source: Authors.

Image 1.7 Mid-sized van used in multiple occupancy as pooled vehicle/taxibus.
Source: Authors.

services. Other examples include trip-specific versions of the shared vehicle concept, such as the Highland Council Transport to Employment service (T2E) and similar wheels to work programmes in the UK.

The concept appears to have regained popularity in recent years, partly as a result of app-based information, with the emergence of TNC 'pool' or 'line' options offered on their booking platforms in some cities. Pool/line appears to be based on the same shared vehicle concepts as the earlier Belfast and Soweto examples of taxibuses and may offer a fare reduction compared with exclusive use of the same vehicle.

Differences in definition do exist, however, often as a result of the original route to market of differing taxibus types. Potential differences visible between services that originated as a development from, or replacement of, a traditional taxi, (Belfast, Soweto, UberPool, etc.); or, alternatively, as a modified form of bus service (Highland Dial-a-bus, etc.). This said, many areas of consistency are visible, discussed in detail in subsequent chapters, with all such services following a shared ride, on-demand concept.

The extent and popularity of different regulations change over time, with quantity constraints and economic controls being frequently subject to review and controversy. Recent developments within the taxi industry created pressures and conflicts between the trade and its regulators, currently dominated by conflicting views in relation to TNCs which can differ in regulatory approach to more traditional operators.

Fares and Fare Measurement

In earlier sections, we highlighted the significance of the taximeter in the development of the mode. The meter provides a reliable measurement of time and distance that may then be applied to a tariff table, typically a published list of distance- and time-based tariffs that are combined to produce a trip-specific fare. Many of the functions of the taximeter can be, and have been, replicated using the location services functions of smartphones, allowing app-based companies to demonstrate adherence to the same principles of tariff, albeit where key variables of distance and time are measured via GPS coordinates.

The measurement of time and distance is necessary but not a sufficient condition for the statement of a fare. The second element is the tariff itself, the stated amount payable for units of distance and/or time. In the case of the traditional taxi, it is likely that a licensing authority will maintain oversight of the tariff, providing public reassurance as to its accuracy, or fairness, and many authorities will be proactive in the determination of amounts which are typically published and displayed in the vehicle and common across all taxis. The review of taxi tariff will often be required under licensing laws, a practice that has spawned a series of taxi cost models, commonly applied at a city level. This approach follows the concept of regulated competition, under which the regulator assumes a role in maintaining a competitively priced market and reducing the potential for anticompetitive price fixing, gouging, or monopolistic market failure.

By contrast, most TNCs and many PHV companies are not subject to the same levels of tariff control. Both PHV companies and, more recently, TNCs have been permitted to define their own tariffs, though often using the same concepts of time and distance, albeit with the requirement to publish fares whether as advertised tables, common in the PHV industry, or via an app as an upfront statement prior to engagement.

Upfront indication of actual trip cost, rather than a statement of mile or time charges, has proven popular amongst app users, giving relative certainty of actual cost, rather than estimated amounts as may be derived from a tariff table without full knowledge of route distance or delays.

Notes

1 Minicabs were introduced in London in regular service from 1963.
2 For hire industry, smartphone applications provide access to a booking and distribution platform through the use of the application (app) in place of more traditional engagement methods. Many apps make use of location services, based on GPS, native to most smartphones. For hire apps maybe subject to differing or additional regulations compared to the traditional taxi industry.
3 For clarity and ease of description, we differentiate between the smartphone application (App) and transport service providers. A further distinction is also necessary between transport service providers that are tied to the app as a primary method of engagement, the transportation network company (TNC), and traditional taxi companies (not TNCs) that offer app-based booking as a part of a wider portfolio of engagement methods.
4 AKA: vehicles for hire (VFHs).
5 AKA: private hire cars (PHCs) (*Scotland*) and car services (*US*).
6 The term hackney is most likely a derivative version of 'Hacquenee', an early French name for an 'ambling nag' (horse) felt suitable to haul carts and carriages. The term is visible in UK literature in the 17th century, appearing in the Diary of Samuel Pepys entry for the day of Thursday 3 August 1665.
7 AKA: sports utility vehicle (SUV).
8 Also described as a wheelchair accessible taxi (WAT) in some locations.
9 As a legal definition of taxi services permitted to ply for hire, for direct on-street engagement (*US: Hailed market*).
10 AKA: Taxi stand / taxi line
11 Reported as following the Wall Street crash of 24th October 1929.
12 The practice of fare or tariff display continues to this day and can be seen in the UK by the legislated requirement to provide a tariff table within vehicles, and the requirement, in the US, to display mile rates on the external panelling and/or decals placed on vehicle windows. Similar requirements exist in many countries.
13 Taxi metering devices used in the USA fall under national, federal, and state Weights and Measures legislation. These are collectively mandated under the control of the US Department of Commerce, National Institute of Standards and Technology (NIST) (Olson, 2020).
14 The mechanical process of applying a tamperproof physical seal to a meter device once calibrated and certified.
15 An example of current regulation includes the Civic Government (Scotland) Act 1982, section on Licensing of Taxis and Private Hire Cars (Scottish Government, 2012).
16 AKA Cruising (*US market*).
17 Synonyms for a taxi rank include taxi stand, taxi stance (*Scotland*), or taxi line (*US*).
18 The term 'Light Taxi Regulation' has been applied to regulatory reforms in some cities, including Saskatoon, Canada.

19 A US term applied in some cities.

20 May include stretched limousines, converted emergency vehicles, and other novelty vehicle types.

21 The US definition of jitney includes shared taxis often following semi-defined routes. US examples of jitney operations include Atlantic City and San Diego. Similar US services are also referred to as Dollar Vans (New York) and the Miami Minibus. In some locations, including the San Diego Metro area, jitneys are recognised to the extent that the city transit agency (The San Diego Metropolitan Transit System [MTS]) provides stop signs, shields, and information placards for jitney use. International examples include public/private light buses and nanny vans in Hong Kong; microbuses in Egypt; share taxi and kombis in South Africa; jeepney in the Philippines; and dolmus in Turkey, amongst others. The term jitney appears to have originated from an archaic name for the US nickel coin (5¢), which may have referred to the fare charged for use.

References

Davis, D.F., (1998) 'The Canadian taxi wars, 1925–1950', *Urban History Review*, 27(1), pp. 7–22.

Gilbert, G. and Samuels, R.E., (1982) *The taxicab: An urban transportation survivor.* Chapel Hill: University of North Carolina Press.

OECD, (2018) *Working party no. 2 on competition and regulation taxi, ride-sourcing and ride-sharing services - Note by the United States* [Online] Available at: https://one.oecd.org/document/DAF/COMP/WP2/WD(2018)27/en/pdf [Accessed 1 August 2022].

Olson, D.D., (2020) National Institute of Standards and Technology. https://www.nist.gov/. [Online] Available at: https://www.nist.gov/system/files/documents/2020/05/27/2021%20Edition%20notice%20final%2020200519_0.pdf [Accessed 1 August 2022].

Scottish Government, (2012) 'Licensing of taxis and private hire cars', *Circular 25/1986*, https://www.gov.scot. [Online] Available at: https://www.gov.scot/publications/circular-25-1986-licensing-taxis-private-hire-cars/ [Accessed 1 August 2022].

Vrkic, L., (2017) All taxi operators. One app. https://www.ingogo.com.au/. [Online] Available at: https://www.ingogo.com.au/blog/a-very-short-history-of-the-taxicab [Accessed 1 August 2022].

2   The Current Market

Today's market might be argued as appearing very different from its historical origins. The market is emerging/has emerged from a pandemic that has challenged many of the operating certainties of the mode and its use. The current market is supported by app technologies, location services at an individual level, and the increasing use of AI algorithms predicting choice behaviours and price responses to an extent not seen in the past. In short, the market faces a very different set of circumstances compared to those present at the outset of regulation in its (more than) 300-year history. And yet, many of the same regulations are present to this day. Many have been argued, both for and against, over the decades and centuries, indeed arguments continue in respect of some of the regulations, arguments related to their strengthening and enhanced application.

What, then, are the roles of the various market participants? What is the role of the regulator in the current market? Do the benefits of continued regulation outweigh the limitations that regulations may place on market development? In short, has the industry developed beyond its historical limitations, or do the underlying justifications for a regulated competitive market remain?

The most visible and substantive changes in the industry are those based on technology and corporate structure, and the most recent disruption from a technology shift associated with the smartphone and its use. But this is not the only change the industry faces. Indeed, it is arguable that the entry of a new technology is anything new. Each step change in the past, whether the motorisation of the industry or the emergence of radio communications, has resulted in a paradigm shift, but not a removal of the quality, quantity, and economic (QQE) structures within which the market operates.

What is new, by contrast, is the confluence of multiple market factors. Not only has the market seen the development of a better dispatch and locations system, but it has also faced a shift in behaviours as a result of COVID. The pandemic contributing to immediate and longer-term structural changes in travel behaviour, and, as the pandemic fades, a change in employment patterns amongst passengers, and in the availability of drivers within the trade. With many countries experiencing acute shortages of vehicle drivers across

DOI: 10.4324/9781003256311-3

the for hire vehicle (FHV) industry, previously inconceivable alliances are beginning to emerge between the bitter rivals of the taxi and transportation network company (TNC) industries.

In the subsequent sections, we discuss a baseline industry structure, the observed evolution of that structure, and the potential effects of the paradigm shifts identified above. It is also appropriate to note that, despite a general view that the FHV industry is broadly consistent, and thus comparable, in many markets, the actual market structure may differ significantly 'below the surface' between locations, complicating the transferability of any lessons that may be learned and removing potential conclusions based on a one-size-fits-all paradigm.

Market Form

In defining the current market, we feel it is important to understand the nature of that market, both in terms of its current and emerging form, and that immediately prior to TNC entry as a baseline. It is also important to outline the fundamental differences between regulated competition, deregulation, de-restriction, and a free market, as each relates to the ability of a market segment to compete and gives rise to the concept of a 'level playing field', a common and current argument associated with fairness or equity, particularly amongst the traditional taxi trade.

The traditional taxi market operates under a form of regulated competition, in which an element of control is applied across one or more elements of its operation. This control is normally allocated to regulators, often the city or district authority, via a series of regulations discussed in more detail in later chapters. The market is competitive, in that multiple suppliers compete for business, but are constrained by the regulations imposed by the regulator. Each regulation is a form of market intervention, a constraint applied through legislation on the free operation of market competition.

Taxi regulations have traditionally been justified as being in the public interest, with some descriptions extending the view that regulation follows from market failure and the inability of the free market to deliver a mutually beneficial/safe outcome in a given set of circumstances. In this analysis, the regulator imposes conditions to the extent as may reasonably approximate a free market and may typically apply a number of tests, tools, or models in that pursuit.

Regulated competition differs from free market competition, in that it applies some controls that would not exist in an unregulated environment, though it needs also to be recognised that all legal markets contain some element of regulation, even if it is simply the recovery of tax or the assurance of minimum safety standards.

The regulation of TNCs differs in that it is more likely to be based on free market principles, with fewer controls on operation, price, or number. These differences have been suggested, by some, to work in the favour of the TNC and to the detriment of the taxi company, insofar as the traditional taxi is subject to a greater, and more onerous, set of controls than the new entrant TNC.

Industry Baseline

By the start of the 21st century, many of the industry's developmental changes, including de-restriction in the US, appeared to have settled into a mature market structure. The industry comprises more highly regulated approaches in larger metropolitan areas, often including quantity constraints, while smaller and more rural communities tended to control for quality and safety standards without defining limits to the number of vehicles permitted to operate. In reality, this absence may also have reflected a paucity in supply, either/both negating the need and/or removing the effectiveness of any such control.

Distinct similarities in regulation existed across international boundaries, likely as a result of similar contexts of supply, though some distinguishing characteristics could be seen, exampled by an increased use of the taxi industry in socially supported transport in northern European markets: an emphasis on multiple occupancy line transport (taxibus) services in and around southern African cities.[1] Localised regional differences are also visible, including the different regulatory structures applied in Northern Ireland, compared to the rest of the UK, and the different approaches between US states, discussed in more detail below.

The period since has seen much of the relative calm of the early 2000s dramatically changed. The Apple iPhone first appeared on the market in 2007, followed by the expansion of location services[2] and the incorporation of GPS-based coordinates into apps. The result being a significantly enhanced and accessible reporting of phone location, both of the (intending) passenger and the vehicle. The expansion of transport apps has not been limited to taxis alone, with a parallel development of transit-oriented apps, and the emergence of digital location mapping, Google Maps[3] in September 2008, Apple Maps from 2012.

While the taxi industry at first appeared reluctant to invest in the app market, it was seen as tangential to or a minor part of their business. TNCs were happy to develop the market segment normally through investment of venture capital into a 'new market'. The TNCs also sought to explicitly avoid the classification of 'taxi' by occupying, in their own words, the space created by 'regulatory ambiguity', initially operating as limousines/town cars in the USA, followed by a shift to non-professional drivers, discussed below. In many instances, the TNC model was not profitable in the short term and appears to have been funded on the basis of its long-term technological potential, similar to the dot com investments common at the outset of app development, rather than on a short turnaround return on investment.

For its part, the traditional industry appeared willing to ignore, or minimise, the development of the TNC market, claiming it was an anomaly that was felt would be corrected over time by the actions of the regulator in re-establishing the ('correctly') regulated order. In so doing, the industry could continue the development of its own apps, albeit as a minor part of their business model, including the launch of TaxiMagic in 2008.[4]

The TNC sector moved quickly to take advantage of the apparent gap. The US market leader, Uber, focused its initial efforts on a parallel 'licensed' service dispatching directly to professional drivers in the private hire vehicle (PHV) market, a service that would be later branded as Uber Black. Competition from Lyft took the market one step further with the company launching its version of the TNC by dispatching directly to non-professional drivers in their own vehicles to provide 'lifts' and share rides. It is likely that public statements of the time alluding to the idea of shared lifts provide a genesis to the inclusion of ridesharing and ridesourcing as definitions, though these both clash with a pre-existing concept of ridesharing, a concept with legal definitions already in use and applied to non-commercial lifts.

The emergence of Lyft and its use of a (cheaper) non-professional fleet prompted a response from its competitor, Uber, which launched a similar service concept, marketed as UberX, also provided by non-professional drivers. Uber also appears to have stolen a march on Lyft, by rushing to market with a launch event held one day prior to that of Lyft. Uber was later to describe the non-professional segment as operating in an area of regulatory ambiguity (Uber, 2013), arguing this to equate '*tacit approval*', though this view has since been refuted in a number of commentaries, including by regulators themselves; alternative interpretations suggested that commencement of UberX operations appeared more related to an absence of direct regulatory opposition rather than specific approval. Collier et al. (2018) defined such entry as occurring where an existing regulatory regime is '*not deregulated but successfully disregarded by a new entrant*'.

The use of non-professional drivers is highly significant as it created a distinctly different environment for regulation. Not least the form of licence appropriate, alongside many questions pertaining to the correct forms of insurance, safety standards, and vehicle testing, formed a backdrop to continued opposition amongst the taxi trade to the newcomers. Similarly, the taxi trade addressed the potential risk to passengers from drivers, as well as that to drivers from passengers, with a series of background checks and driver safety features. Such features were less focused on by new entrant TNCs, suggesting that the information held on both driver and passenger would allow actions to be taken, but equally was seen as less substantive than the rigorous checks required of the taxi industry. It is arguable whether these represented the actual difficulties that were associated with them but remained a diversion from a more market-oriented response of taxi app development. It is notable that, in many cases, TNC and taxi background checks appear to have moved closer to each other.

The Market since 2020

Today's FHV market, at least that visible at the time of writing, sits awkwardly between the long-established taxi mode and the emergent TNC. The conflict is visible and often palpable, as the traditional taxi trade appears hesitant, and potentially unable, to fully address its competitor, while the TNC sector continues to push at the boundaries, both operational and legal.

While this, almost inevitably, describes the market in terms of generalities, it appears broadly the case that the taxi has not kept up with its TNC competition. Observable differences include the range and scale of services offered by the two, the TNC expanding its delivery platform to accommodate non-passenger services, effectively treating the driver and vehicle as a capital resource, resulting in a range of freight and food transport options available from the TNC side. Similar moves for the taxi industry appear sporadic and poorly coordinated, though this might in turn be a result of the atomistic nature of the taxi industry compared to the centralised management structures of TNCs. Education and/or NEMT contracts, while common amongst the traditional taxi industry, are typically a localised service, often in response to an authority RFT.[5] TNCs can offer more significant and scaled transport, in contrast, and may include the large-scale provision of paratransit services, sometimes as a named TNC 'transit' service, and supported by a significantly larger back office than possible within the traditional industry, as seen in the instance of the Boston MBTA Ride Flex programme,[6] and bespoke booking platforms.

Non-passenger transport services within the taxi industry appear minor compared to the same programmes offered by the TNCs. Examples include freight carriage, parcel delivery, and food delivery, though the concept of pizza delivery was already an established market share, and even the established use of the term 'pizza taxi' in some German locations. The latter 'delivery/grub/eats' services represent a significant market segment, with a significant growth in its own right over the pandemic as more households chose to have restaurant food delivered home. Small parcel delivery might also fall into this segment, despite an established delivery network amongst multi-national courier services but has yet to make significant inroads outside of limited 'city-logistics' concepts.

Other 'innovations[7]' observed from the TNC side include shared (pool) and line-based services (Lyft Line, Uber Pool, and similar), picking up many of the shared occupancy possibilities of taxibus services/jitneys in the USA. These appear to be aimed at competing with, rather than being complementary to, transit services. The cross-sectoral term mobility as a service (MaaS) may also apply to the segment, though this is poorly defined as a service and is more frequently used to describe cross-operator platforms outwit TNC control. This said, some examples of multi-operator platforms that include TNCs are visible, including in New York, also carrying MaaS and/or accessibility branding and dispatching to multiple companies on the basis of passenger benefit/operational efficiencies.

In recent discussions, the issue of FHV contribution to congestion has also been raised. Two factors appear to be in play: the first is the rapid growth in vehicles in FHV use, created by the entry of TNCs to the market; the second is diversionary effects caused by mass public transport options to the FHV mode. While each city is likely to differ, in part as a result of the strength of incumbent taxi and/or public transport operators, some common themes are visible. The first element, that of increased vehicle numbers, is likely to be true in most cities. This may not represent a real-term increase in the total vehicle parc, that is, the total number of cars may remain similar, but rather their use, as measured by vehicle kilometres, will increase rapidly to reflect the adoption of the same vehicle from private use to use as an FHV. More worryingly, perhaps, the diversion of public transport trips to FHV trips. The latter observed in the case of passenger use of bus vehicles, a relatively environmentally friendly vehicle where congestion and polluting effects could be divided by the total (and now declining) number of passengers, being replaced by an additional marginal trip in a more polluting vehicle,[8] multiplied by the number of diverted trips. FHVs, of most types, will also likely engage in cruising, whereby a driver will circulate around city streets in search of a passenger, the so-called 'plying for hire'. These trips can also be referred to as 'dead miles', as no passenger is present, while still contributing to congestion and pollution.

Atomised Markets and Lobbying

Much of the growth of the TNC, and its apparent ability to adopt and steal a march on its traditional taxi rival, reflect the relative ability of the 'sides' to communicate and lobby for their respective positions.

For its part, the TNC industry appears to have focused its early establishment around communications, including the development of a strong lobbying position, supported by the inherent popularity of its platform amongst smartphone users. The TNC mode may also have benefitted from the relative size of its companies, having invested heavily on the back of their 'technology status', resulting in heavily indebted companies with (very) large organisational reach, lobbying power, and international presence. The extent of TNC lobbying indicative of an economy of scale in communications, that could not be matched by any single taxi operator. This said, not all locations are seen to respond to industrial lobbying in the same way. The potential existing for the message to be lost, or diminished, in translation; while some locations may go further to suggest that 'things are not done like that here'.

The taxi operator, in contrast, has generally focused on local markets. Individual cities are served to be a number of competing taxi 'companies',[9] comprising many independent drivers and often competing with an even greater number of independent 'street taxi' operators not affiliated with the taxi companies in their location. The result of which has been an atomised taxi industry with a lower level of coordination or common messaging compared to their TNC competitor, making the taxi companies vulnerable to being out lobbied, portrayed negatively as an incumbent, and unable to (individually) offer the same app-based service compared to the newcomer.

Perceptions of service quality can also differ between the competitors, while a lack of coordination within the taxi industry can contribute to dissatisfaction, often based on a passenger's experience of a bad trip. Taxi companies are poorly placed to visibly respond to such experiences, while the regulator, having the role of defining standards, may also be seen as responding slowly or without power. The TNC, in contrast, appears to have a higher level of trust amongst its users, above that attributed to their taxi competitors, and, critically, a higher level of trust in the TNC than in the taxi regulator. TNC ratings contribute positively to passenger perceptions, with the same system providing a rapid and effective response to bad service amongst drivers.

For their part, the TNCs have been active in self-promotion, often presenting the taxi competition as an unresponsive 'big industry', while pushing their own development above and beyond the inherent limitations of the incumbent. Arguments are also apparent in terms of the power of the regulator, with accusations of regulatory capture not uncommon, particularly in North America. European arguments, in contrast, have related to the distinct nature of the TNC sitting beyond, and thus outwith, traditional regulation. The nature of this argument appears to differ by location, though the larger TNCs have made arguments that their development coincides with a period of 'regulatory ambiguity' created, in part, by their presence, and implying a lack of a regulatory structure rather than an unwillingness to comply with one.

The regulators also face a number of issues in the nature of controls applied to the market. The traditional model of regulation, a series of controls applied to the QQE of the industry, had developed and existed as appropriate to public needs prior to the emergence of the TNC. Regulations were broadly focused on local needs and administered by city and district governments (*municipal regulation*) rather than at the larger regional and national scale of the new market entrants. Immediate conflicts emerged where cities defined local regulation in respect of a subset of the operational area of a new entrant, including and not least the requirement that local offices be maintained by companies that were, by design, virtual, national, and/or multi-national in their operation.

By seeking to maintain and promote an existing structure, the regulators could be painted as opposing the advancement of the TNC newcomer and as supporting the needs, direction, or interest of the taxi competition, the basis of an accusation of regulatory capture. The outcome was that regulators stood to be illustrated as against the development/advancement of the industry, as opposing its technologies, and worse, being in the enthral of the incumbent industry. In this way, the regular could be suggested as operating in bad faith and/or against the public interest.[10] In this light, regulation was a barrier to the operation of the market, rather than its facilitator, being the stated ideal applied prior to the emergence of the TNC. The argument was also supported by the proactive nature of some TNCs, itself a further factor in the apparent conflict between traditional and emerging operators.

Market Segments

In the preceding chapter, we identified that many of the regulations applied to the FHV industry could be traced to specific events over time, with a number reflecting significant histories. By the early 2000s, the taxi market began to face new technologies and new challengers seeking to develop the information and communications technology (ICT) options appearing in the market. Online platforms became popular, though initially based on Internet access, with app developments to follow as the phone technologies advanced in capability and popularity.

The introduction of the app as a method of booking and dispatch has changed the dynamics of the industry but not its fundamentals. This said, the various approaches adopted have led to a series of market structures that can, loosely, be applied and transferred between locations. In the following chapters, we will describe the social and economic impacts that follow from the market models, their theoretical grounding, and the practical observable impacts by passenger and stakeholder groups.

At this point, however, we define market models as pertaining to each visible supply segment.

* FHV market

    We define the FHV market as a generic title for all vehicles for hire. The term is frequently used interchangeably with the vehicle for hire (VFH) market, and we will assume the intended use is the same. The market can also be described, generically, as 'the taxi market', though we recognise the potential for confusion in this use.

    The FHV market is almost always operated privately, by individuals, groupings, or cooperatives, creating additional markets between operators, including taxi dispatch companies, TNCs, private hire cars (PHCs), and their drivers. A range of terms are applied to the dispatch organisations, which include 'taxi companies', 'brokers', 'dispatch platforms', and similar, all with the role of mediating requests for transport (demand) and its provision (supply).

    An intermediate level may also exist, being the owner of vehicles, who may also 'own' the requisite licence, plate, and permit but need not do so. Vehicle owners can be referred to as operators and will sometimes include drivers – driver operators. Drivers without their own vehicles may rent or share vehicles and may work specific shifts for an operator or a garage. It is normal that the day-to-day risk of provision is taken by the driver, while operators may take investment risks where permits carry an inherent tradable value.

- TNC market segment

  With the exception of consolidator and MaaS platforms, the TNC is the newcomer to the FHV market. It can be described as having the smallest access to the market, insofar as it is (generally) limited to app-based bookings alone, but this may in turn give a misleading picture. The TNC sector is also the least regulated of the FHV providers and is subject to lower levels of control, including an absence of fare regulation, again as a general statement, and lower entry requirements in many locations compared to many of its traditional competitors.

  The TNC segment is also likely to be the most frequently used vehicle type with most large cities reporting multiples of user numbers than the traditional taxi. Effectively, the TNC has proven highly popular amongst a growing user base, for whom the use of an app does not represent an impediment to use.

  While not entirely absent, authority intervention on price is limited, often to the requirement that users are made aware of trip costs in advance of travel. As a result, a majority of TNCs operate a system of variable pricing, advised on booking, including the application of trip cost supplements also known as 'surge pricing' stated as responsive to a lack of supply, the additional fares being charged to encourage supply. In periods of surge pricing, the TNC fare will often exceed that of its taxi competitor, but with little price competition effect as a result of the point in a booking process at which the fare is displayed.[11]

  The TNC industry has also faced scrutiny over its driver checking and insurance requirements, though these are largely historic in nature.

- PHCs market

  The market for PHCs[12] is an intermediate categorisation broadly applied to taxi-like vehicles that are available for pre-booking alone. The PHC sector emerged as an in-fill broadly justified as necessary where taxi services were in heavy demand, but insufficient arguments could be made to justify an increase in taxi numbers.

  The PHC sector faces many of the same regulatory requirements as the traditional taxi but is less likely to be fully controlled in terms of fares, able to define and publish their own fares in many instances. The PHC segment is also limited in terms of its permitted pickup behaviour, being more akin to the TNC industry than the taxi industry, typically requiring pre-booking, or base dispatch as a method of engagement, and being unable to pick up on flagging.

  As in the TNC sector, the PHC is able to use apps, as well as phone and office-based booking, but has not achieved the level of market share seen in the TNC sector.

- Taxi/hackney carriage market

  Taxis are permitted to pick up passengers across all three of the primary engagement methods, by hailing (plying for hire), at taxi stands, and by dispatch. The market segment is frequently given exclusive access to the hailed market, being unavailable to both TNC and PHC competitors. This said, the taxi will often be subject to greater regulatory controls than its competitors, partly as a result of its exclusive access to the hail market, alongside the official / regulated definition of tariff rates. The imposition of fares is most frequently justified on the basis of a lack of competition amongst taxis, described as situational or instant monopolies in some accounts.

The taxi segment is also more likely to face quantity controls, typically a limitation on the number of licences issued, than other market segments, though this is not universally the case, with examples of locations not applying quantity caps to taxis (e.g. London) and those where caps are applied to both the taxi and the PHC sector (e.g. Glasgow). The sector is also subject to the most stringent quality controls, such as vehicle and driver fitness tests, including the 'London knowledge', a well-known example of geographic and local knowledge test applied to the taxi sector.

• Conflicts, anomalies, and surprises

The development of the PHV industry, particularly in response to app development, has created a series of competitive and contradictory pressures. It is undoubtedly the case that app services have expanded the total market for PHVs, although this growth has not been even across the segments.

Image 2.1 Marked taxi rank in Brussels.
Source: Authors.

Responses have followed a number of different patterns, explored in more detail in the following chapters, including the protection of the hail sector for the traditional taxi, although the emergence of apps as a significantly more accurate location service has largely diluted this as a benefit to the taxi industry. In some locations, including New York, the hail market is explicitly extended to include 'e-hailing', the permitted use of defined apps for immediate street corner hails of direct equivalence to the plying for hire hailed market and a popular alternative giving the heavy demand for hailed yellow cabs in the Manhattan district of the city. The New York example demonstrates the use of apps in a traditional hailed market and its theoretical transfer to all taxi markets.

The exit from the COVID pandemic has also created a number of surprises. Not least is the emerging collaboration between TNCs and the taxi industry, specifically taxi dispatching app providers, to allow TNC app users to access taxis on the same platform. The TNC/taxi link is not entirely new, having been used in previous iterations to provide accessible vehicles but is new in its direct application to traditional TNC trips, likely a result of a lack of drivers and discussed in more detail below.

Notes

1 South African townships provide a good example of jitney operation, being shared taxis operating in a similar pattern to bus services along defined routes and charging individual separate fares. See Woolf and Joubert (2013) for a description of current jitney and paratransit services in South Africa.
2 The Benefon Esc! was the first handheld smartphone to include a GPS function, launched in 1999 (https://www.geotab.com/blog/gps-satellites/), while the mass market Samsung i550 was launched in 2007 and the iPhone 3G in 2008 (https://www.citymac.com/blog/2013/09/02/ios-gps-and-location-services).
3 PC-oriented versions of Google Maps was launched in 2005.
4 Taxi Magic operated as an extension of the RideCharge web platform resource (2008), initially intended as a fare-charging resource.
5 Requests for tenders (RFT), AKA: request for proposal (RFP) or request for quote (RFQ), are reactive, where the taxi company responds to a call for contracted FHV services, such as the transportation of school pupils. They are typically confined to a small area or single-line services.
6 https://www.mbta.com/accessibility/the-ride/on-demand-pilot (Accessed 1 August 2022).
7 Taxi-based approaches to line and pooled TNC services are visible and usually predate their TNC versions. Examples include taxibus services across southern Africa, Black Taxi and taxibus in the UK, particularly focused on Belfast, Northern Ireland; the transport to employment (T2E) service operated in the Highland council area of Scotland; and various postbus and DRT initiatives elsewhere.
8 The issue of total pollutants is significant at this point. While it is clear that a passenger saloon vehicle is likely to create less pollutants and congestion than a bus vehicle, its actual effect needs to be measured on a per-passenger basis. The diversion from busses to FHVs, thus reducing the number of passengers per bus, has the double impact of making per-bus passenger impacts worse and adding further congestion and pollution from the FHV trip. A counterweight argument

can be made where trips are diverted from private cars, making single trips, to the more effective use of a collective car (the FHV) making multiple trips. The extent to which one balances out the other will be location specific and reflect local priority and traffic management measures.

9 The definition of a taxi company is highly variable and will often differ within as well as between countries. The fundamental role of the taxi company is the dispatch of trips amongst its 'members', with many taxi companies based on collaborative operation and cooperative or association corporate structures.

10 A series of articles address regulatory capture as a form of anticompetitive pressure, traced (Novak, 2013) to business practices emerging from the second World War, defined as 'capture theses'.

11 The incentive to seek competitive prices is lessened as the process for booking advances, comparable to a 'first screen effect' observed in the aviation industry and implying a high value of time (assumed time) in comparison.

12 AKA: Private hire vehicles (PHVs), minicabs, Black Cars, limousines (not luxury), car services. The term 'jitney' is applied to the PHC sector in the Republic of Ireland but this differs from the use of the term 'jitney' in the USA.

References

Collier, R., Dubal, V. and Carter, C., (2018) 'Disrupting regulation, regulating disruption: The politics of Uber in the United States', *Perspectives on Politics*, 16(4), pp. 919–937.

Novak, W.J., (2013) 'A revisionist history of regulatory capture', in Carpenter, D. and Moss, D.A. (eds) *Preventing regulatory capture: Special interest influence and how to limit it*. Cambridge: Cambridge University Press, pp. 25–48. doi:10.1017/CBO9781139565875.004

Uber, (2013) 'Principled innovation—Addressing the regulatory ambiguity', *Uber White Paper 1.0*. Available at: https://www.benedelman.org/uber/uber-policy-whitepaper.pdf

Woolf, S.E. and Joubert, J., (2013) 'A people-centred view on paratransit in South Africa', *Cities*, 35, pp. 284–293. doi:10.1016/j.cities.2013.04.005

3 Taxis in Culture

While much of our concentration must focus on the technical, operational, and regulatory aspects of the industry, a significant area of cultural significance should also be considered. Neither should the two aspects be completely separated. References made to the mode, from the earliest inclusion of hansom cabs in the stories of Sherlock Holmes to the presentations of technologies, and an increasing indication of the competing roles of taxis and transportation network companies (TNCs), references made to uber-ing rather than taxi-ing, provide a picture, albeit temporary, of the role of the mode at the time of the reference.

Images and icons also inform the perception of the intending user, a fact likely to hold across many industries. What is fashionable will receive more attention than what is not. Behavioural emulation can also be suggested as a major benefit arising from presentation, while affection, often associated with, what has become known as, influencer impact, itself closely associated with app-based technologies. While the traditional industry can be associated with particular patterns, behaviours, and icons, not always positively, the use of pattern, social positioning, even public perceptions, and use of the industry may follow from its appearance on a silver screen, in song lyrics, or as blogged about by influencers, all adding to the mode's/modes' part(s) of the cultural zeitgeist of the time.

The last 125 years, albeit a rough estimate, have seen the emergence of a motorised taxi. The period has created many iconic symbols, some easy to see, but often overlooked, some apparently obscure but instantly recognisable. Examples include the colour yellow; a chequered band; a roof sign, a roof light, or a roof dome if you prefer, all examples of service identifiers unique to the industry. Other examples include, in London, an iconic and recognisable vehicle body shape; in the US, a series of regulatory markers, including physical medallion plates etc.

A significant number of immediate identifiers appear first in the 1920s and 1930s, and a fair number were created alongside each other. John Hertz, of the rental car company fame, shaped the 'look' of the US taxi trade early on, including the adoption of the yellow color scheme, giving rise to the Yellow Cab brand. Yellow felt to be an easily visible colour for vehicles in dusk and at night.

DOI: 10.4324/9781003256311-4

The current day accessibility of the London fleet is rumoured to have followed from an initial requirement that the vehicle accommodate the need for a gentleman to wear a tall top hat inside the vehicle, a fortuitous outcome being the extended height of the London taxi vehicle that remains to this day. The coincidence allowed the vehicle to be sufficiently large to accommodate wheelchairs when these became more important than millinery alone.

The developments were not a one-way street. The trade has put a distinctive stamp on life beyond the industry, colouring parts of daily life which have little or no direct connection with the taxi industry. Taxi originating terms used outside the taxi industry may, in reality, be unrelated to the actual role of the taxi, while other transport uses, notably the action of an aeroplane in accessing its stand, appear only partially associated with the physical ground movement of its erstwhile predecessor. In this chapter, we'll show the development of specific socio-cultural markers within the industry and in wider society with specific references from the TV, film, and music industry.

Early History

Prior to the existence of a motorised vehicle, the industry was focused on horse-drawn transport. Very early excursions into human motive power, around the hand-carried Chaise a Bras, appear an unrealistic form of mass transportation. Hackney carriages, believed to have been named after the French term for cart-pulling horses, had already left their indelible mark on street life and society. Growlers and similar rudimentary carts were followed by distinct and ultra-modern hansom cabs, of unique appearance and gaining a significant reputation in the Victorian streets of London. Their use suggested in the works of Sir Arthur Conan Doyle as an everyday occurrence, as experienced by the fictional detective Sherlock Holmes, and presumably by the very real readers of the Strand Magazine in which his exploits were chronicled.

Horses gave way to the very earliest of electric vehicles, Bersey electric cabs distinct by their homing sound, and possibly their unreliability. The electric vehicle was followed by one of the most distinctive of taxis, the Carbodies petrol- or diesel-powered taxi in London, recognisable both by the service type offered, and by the shape of their vehicles.

Structured taxi ranks, like the first one which appeared in London in 1634 at the Maypole on the Strand and the one in Paris which operated from 1637 outside the shrine to Saint Fiacre, were clear and early indications of the nascent industry, the stand itself a point of controversy, both loved and disliked at the same time. The developing industry sought unique appearances, drivers being dressed in uniforms with both drivers and vehicles adopting distinct uniform and livery markings. The very first ranking taxis, operated by Captain John Bailey, would follow strict rules for what drivers could charge and be subject to a code of conduct for his employees.

The emerging ranks would be accompanied by Cabman's shelters, now referred to as bothies amongst the UK taxi trade. Sixty were built in and

Image 3.1 London Cabmans' Bothy.
Source: Authors.

around St John's Wood from 1875 onwards, with a remarkable 13 remaining to this day to provide shelter, and tea, to passing taxi drivers. The bothies continue to enforce the strict rules of conduct first applied over 100 years prior: no swearing, gaming, gambling, or drinking alcohol!

Technologies have also been a key part of the development of the industry. Different vehicle types were joined by advances in communication. The telephone would be joined in the 1950s by radio-based communication, improving the quality and speed of dispatch and creating a step change, possibly even a revolution in the structure of the industry. The radio created a need for radio circuits, booking centres, and cab companies, while the development and success of apps can be linked to the popularity and widespread use of smartphones.

Identity and Belonging

Since its start, the taxi industry has developed not only outward markings of vehicles and ranks but also an 'esprit de corps', a series of understandings and symbols by which it is recognisable and a sense of camaraderie between those involved in the trade: drivers, operators, and support personnel. It has also incorporated and shared a series of formal and informal professional standards and uses. We will return to these symbols in a moment but would make the point that the symbolism, markings, and vehicles used, all enhance this camaraderie, the feeling of belonging to a distinctive trade with clear behavioural roles. The London industry providing a good example has built up an impressive array of expressions, often only used with taxi meanings and understood by those active in the trade. Quite a few are very humorous. But this separate 'taxi language' is not exclusive to the London taxi trade and can be found almost everywhere in the trade.

'Be lucky' in this 'random' industry based on the lucky draw of the next passenger is still a well-known and well-used greeting in the London trade. A 'bilker' is a person who doesn't pay his fare, and a 'butter boy/girl' is new to the trade, having just passed the knowledge, the strict entry exam applied to London hackney carriage drivers. Local terms can exist for places: the 'gas works' are the London Houses of Parliament, while distinct terms for different characters can also be seen, a 'musher' is a taxi driver who owns his one vehicle, a 'roader' is a long trip, and a 'flyer' is a passenger to the airport. There are many more, as there are several dictionaries for this particular industry language.

These trade expressions are not limited to London – there are quite a few interesting examples from other languages. They tend to be quite descriptive. For instance, Berlin taxi drivers often call their roof sign 'Fackel' (Eng.: torch), and when lit, looking for work, it is called a 'Hungerlampe' (Eng.: hunger light) of taxi drivers hungry for work. The wealth of expressions is a testament to the longevity of the taxi trade. The fact that the word 'taxi', 'taxis', 'taxicab', 'cabdriver', and 'hackdriver' are recognised Scrabble-words adds anecdotal proof to that long history.

The taxi industry has also coloured much of the socio-cultural world beyond the trade by exporting words from the taxi industry or forming a (tenuous) link with it. Fast for delivery in Germany provides an example, with home delivery of food sometimes referred to using a taxi epithet, such as the 'pizza taxi' in the 1970s.

Two fascinating and different examples of extra-industry use of the word taxi (for instance) were 'taxi dancer' and 'taxi squad', whereby the latter had a connection to the taxi industry. Interestingly, both expressions hail from the last century – the 1920s and 1940s, respectively – but are still used to this day. Historically, the term taxi dancers referred to women who would dance with men in the American dancehalls of a century ago, collecting paid tickets at a dime each in order to earn a commission from the venue. You can get a pretty good picture of the terms from the 1931 film 'Ten Cents a Dance'.

'Taxi squad' is an American football expression with true taxi roots. The taxi squad is an approach that allows you to 'stash' players off the active roster while earning playing time in the National Football League (NFL). These are typically rookies or second-year players. The word dates back to the 1940s, and most professional US football teams have at least one such player. The taxi squads became even more popular at times of epidemic outbreak as players were able to be able to step in at short notice, to replace their ill colleagues. The term was first coined during the 1940s by the Cleveland Browns football team. Coach Paul Brown invented the term when he wanted to hang on to a group of promising players who didn't make the first team. He didn't want to lose them, so the Cleveland Browns owner Arthur McBride put them on the payroll of his taxi company – Cleveland Yellow Cab Co. That's how the term taxi squad was born and would ultimately be adopted by the NFL.

Vehicle Appearance

While language, liveries, ranks, and other industry identifiers have had a significant role in establishing a taxi identity, it is the appearance of a clearly recognisable vehicle that creates a visual identity for the trade. Shape and appearance are significant across all of the taxi market classifications, including private hire, aka minicabs in London. Less immediate markers include signage and discrete markers, including the TNC market, exampled by distinct lighted signs, required external badges and vehicle stickers, referred to as 'decals' in North America. The extent of required, and legislated, visibility will differ between segments, where vehicle markings are less necessary for identification purposes, such as the private hire vehicle (PHV) segment; as PHVs did not and cannot rank or ply for hire, fewer regulatory markings may be required. The external markings are based on both regulatory requirement and pragmatic need. A passenger awaiting a pre-booked vehicle, for example, has a need to identify that vehicle, potentially differentiating their ride from a number of others. Airport pick-up zones are an example of the need, where multiple passengers wait to choose from multiple vehicles, and the need is further enhanced.

Physical demonstrations of a licensed status have also entered common parlance, medallions, small pieces of shaped aluminium physically stapled to New York taxis, popular mementos, or at least indicative symbols of value. For marketing purposes, vehicles regularly advertise the name and phone number of the service, while some cities are typified by particular vehicle body shapes and/or vehicle colours. Some cities in the US, particularly those on the west coast, have established corporate identity by colour, with regulatory requirements to maintain company-specific appearances, aka 'color schemes'.

The newly categorised 'minicabs', introduced in London in 1961, were not only 'mini' but also launched a distinctive style with the use of smaller vehicles compared to the standard taxi. The London hackney carriage market is being dominated by the five-seater Austin Carbodies FX3 and FX4, aka the 'London taxi'. The minicab is operated, in contrast, by Ford Anglias, Renault Dauphines, and similar vehicles hitherto not known for paid transportation on London's streets. Their brazen contrast, made possible by a loophole in the law, upset the existing taxi industry used to having a virtual monopoly in its area. London's first 'minicab wars' broke out in 1961 with significant regulatory argument and recrimination, a possible portend of things to come.

Sixty years ago, London experienced a minor revolution, thanks to the Wimbledon firm of Carline. Its fleet of Ford Anglia 105Es became the capital's first minicabs, and they carried 500 passengers in the first week of operation. The company had exploited a loophole in the 1869 Carriage Act, claiming that these 'cabs' would not be plying for hire but would operate by responding to calls made to its main office and then relayed by radio link to the driver. The 1963 film *Carry-on Cabby* illustrated the conflict between the old guard and new entrant taxi fleets. Later. 25 black-and-white liveried Fiat Multiplas – in use as proper taxis in Italy – joined the minicab fleet, as the two-door Anglias proved rather inconvenient for passengers getting in and out. It was the introduction of a fleet of 800 bright-red Renault Dauphines run by car rental firm Welbeck Motors that caused a sensation on London's streets and became the public face of the minicab. Apart from relying on the income from passengers, Welbeck also sold advertising space on these Dauphines for £75 a week.

Regulatory requirements have also played a role in the appearance and design of vehicles used. The 1906 Conditions of Fitness, set by the regulatory Public Carriage Office (London) and applied to the London hackney carriage fleet, defined minimum vehicle standards, including a 25-feet (7.62 m.) turning circle and minimum ground clearance that were likely to be met by a small number of vehicle types and designs alone. The result being the development of the Carbodies vehicle described above and a continuation of a very recognisable, you could say iconic, London taxi design ever since. The most recent incarnation is the Electric TX taxi manufactured by the London Electric Vehicle Company (LEVC).

Similarly, the 1950s Checker taxicab, produced by the Checker Cab Manufacturing Company in Kalamazoo, Michigan, became ubiquitous between 1956 and 1982 (when production ceased) as the standard vehicle in the US taxi industry. The vehicle met New York City's 1929 ordinance that all taxis must be able to carry five passengers behind a partition and be equipped with high doors allowing passengers easy and considerably more graceful access. The vehicles were fitted with a pair of jump seats to allow them to meet the five-passenger requirement. Both vehicles, the London and Checker taxis, were popular for the space they offered passengers.

There were (and are) other classic taxi models, of which the Indian Hindustan Ambassador, still a staple taxi on the Indian streets (despite its ceasing production in 2014), is the most well known. These models were not conceived or built as taxis but became favourites of taxi operators for their ruggedness and durability. In the US, the Checker cab was followed by the Ford Crown Victoria, often as a used vehicle purchased from police fleets: now replaced by the Toyota Prius, the latter often used for its comparative fuel efficiency. In Japan, the Toyota Crown Sedan and Comfort appear to be long-time staple taxis, while Mercedes-Benz taxis are particularly common in their home market in Germany and in various guises and vintages in different countries.

Recent history has brought immediate recognition to yellow cabs, as one of the hallmarks of city life in New York City. The same is true for the black taxis in London, which, alongside the classic bright-red buses, have defined London's streetscape, including in film and television portrayals thereof. While need, availability, and regulations have changed, the iconic images have not. London's black taxis need no longer be black but retain the name; while the yellow Checker cab has been replaced by more modern vehicle types, the image and portrayal remain. Drivers, too, retain portrayal in distinct lights, the New York driver being something of a tough guy, the London driver as capable and likely to engage in long conversations about whatever passes their vision or enters their mind.

Uniform images and distinct appearances include colours, 'yellow taxis' across the US, 'black cabs' in the UK, and a required taxi-specific light ivory, in Germany, at one time obligatory in its use. The combination of black and yellow has become a typical combination for the taxi trade in various European countries. Other colour codes – often used briefly – sometimes had a somewhat hilarious effect: in the 1960s, Amsterdam taxicabs had to have a hard-orange roof, even though the actual cab had a completely different colour. As if the orange roof was not enough, besides a standard unified roof sign, the chequered band ran alongside the side of the taxi vehicle, not exactly making for an attractive picture. The taxicabs even adopted the (Dutch) name of this black and white chequered band: Blokband taxi translated to and with significant links to the US 'chequered band –taxi'. In Portugal, taxi roofs were painted a green colour, known locally in Lisbon as the colour of the sea. Washington DC adopted a uniform red to match the city's local transport colours and in so doing sought to link taxis to the local transport 'offer'.

Key Players, John Hertz

While it is clearly the case that colours have emerged, updated, and been justified against a series of (different) criteria, one person can be attributed with a significant influence. John Daniel Hertz laid much of the groundwork for the professional taxi industry we know today.

John Hertz has two related areas of fame. He is widely known for the rent-a-car business which later bore his name and is still present globally to this day but was highly influential in the development of the organised taxi industry.

Hertz, a native of what is now Slovakia, emigrated with his family to the US when he was three years old, developing a series of work experiences leading to car sales, a craze in the US at the time. Hertz sought to innovate and revolutionise, introducing the concept of free roadside service at any hour, probably necessary, as cars were notoriously unreliable, but a unique sales pitch at the time. Further innovations included the trade in of older, used, cars, a novelty in 1907, challenging the company, a seller of new cars alone, with the issue of what to do with the older cars taken in part exchange.

Image 3.2 John Hertz.
Source: Authors.

The solution was to use them as livery cars, the forerunner to the limou-sine market in 1910s Chicago. Used cars could be hired, with driver, by the hour or day. City taxicabs were also emerging, with Hertz proposing the rental of excess cars together with a driver for specific clients. Hertz won the concession to provide ten cars to the Chicago Athletic Association and later launched a livery-specific business, the Walden W. Shaw Auto Livery Company. In 1909, the Shaw company provided 30 cabs to the luxurious new LaSalle Hotel, merging, in 1910, with the City Motor Cab Company. The new company started to order custom-made, larger, and more rugged durable cars for its use as taxi, expanding its fleet of cars and service garages around Chicago. Between 1913 and 1914, Hertz not only travelled to Europe, as a rest, but also allowed the study of European taxi systems, with lessons to take back to the US.

In 1915, Hertz chose a yellow for the cabs that stood out most in the streets of Chicago (reportedly also particularly at night), changing the company brand name to Yellow Cab and paying drivers more, with stipulated cour-tesy and skills required. He stabilised and improved drivers' rights, and their incomes, while also going through an intense training programme: drivers were required to dress in company uniforms, shine their shoes, and clean their cars after every customer. Hertz also gave them 20% of the profits of the company and provided the drivers with access to medical care and legal assistance. Drivers were not allowed to work on their cars – for that Hertz had company-owned garages and repair shops.

In 1921, Shaw and Hertz created a separate company, the Yellow Cab Manufacturing Company, to specialise in taxicabs, trucks, and buses.

The manufacturing company became an immediate success, with continually rising stock on the stock market. In 1923, Hertz acquired 'Jacobs DriveUrSelf' and renamed it 'Hertz DriveUrSelf', the precursor to the Hertz company known today, although the latter, Hertz rental, along with the manufacturing company were in fact sold to General Motors in 1925. In 1929, Hertz sold all his taxi interests to Morris Markin, the owner of the Checker Cab Company, who merged both companies but kept the different liveries. Interestingly, Markin started building the large, sturdy, and well-known Checker cabs and private vehicles in Kalamazoo, Michigan, well into the 1950s the main taxi vehicle – and one of the taxi industry's cultural icons – in the USA.

The Taxi as a Cultural Icon in TV and Film

While remaining and consolidating their actual role as a staple for transport, a reel role has also emerged for the iconic taxi.

The American TV series *Taxi* ran for nearly five years from 12 September 1978 to 6 May 1982, on ABC and later from 30 September 1982 to 15 June 1983, on NBC. The film 'Taxi Driver' was released in 1976, with similar titles across many countries and many languages.

The sitcom *Taxi* focused on the everyday lives of a handful of New York City cab drivers, a truly motley crew, bossed around by their abusive dispatcher. No doubt based on real-life experiences in the New York industry of the time, the series garnered no less than 18 Emmy Awards. Its activity is focused on a fleet garage, the Sunshine Cab Company, typical of New York taxis of the time. Drivers Alex Reiger (Judd Hirsch), Bobby Wheeler (Jeff Conaway), Elaine Nardo (Marilu Henner), Tony Banta (Tony Danza), and 'Reverend' Jim Ignatowski (Christopher Lloyd) appeared rugged and smart, 'wise guys' if you like. The garage being the domain of the dictatorial dispatcher Louie De Palma (Danny DeVito)., and focused on the relationships, of each, and need for the other, with comic interaction from the outlandishly foreign mechanic Latka Gravas (Andy Kaufman).

The format became popular, the taxi vehicle allowing a range of interactions. The US sitcom transferred to Dutch TV with great success, forcing its producers to appoint more actors as would-be taxi drivers. The format was further sold to several countries and won the press award at the Rose d'Or Festival for amusement programmes in Montreux in 1995. In 2020, the format ran again on Dutch TV (SBS6) and in 2022 on Belgian TV (VRT). Similar programmes also followed, with *Taxicab Confessions* and *Cash Cab* being examples of a format using hidden cameras and microphones. Drivers chatting with passengers could present very personal narratives that had become more intrusive than in *Taxi*, with people talking about highs and lows in their lives and romantic encounters. *Cash Cab*, originally a UK format, was a totally different programme, compared to the original *Taxi* programme or *Taxicab Confessions*, mixing elements of a game show with the moving taxicab.

The big screen also has its fair share of taxis. Everyone recognises the concept of the taxi, with most recognising its key imagery often across national borders. One use of a cab is to link different scenes via passengers who are arriving or departing. In some cases, for whatever reason, it can be a bonus that taxis are relatively unobtrusive or unnoticeable in city street scenes. Another use of the taxicab is in so-called 'exposition scenes'. A character sitting in the back of a taxi can provide essential information to the audience. In films, taxi drivers often ask questions: 'Where are you going?', 'What do you do for a living', 'Are you new to the city?'. The filmmaker informs the audience about a new development. Not only is the (main) character on the move (if the main character is not the taxi driver), but he or she also provides hints which may be useful further on in the film.

When two people – who are not on good terms – are 'trapped', closely together, in a taxi, these rides can be fairly intense. In the confined space of a cab, it is difficult not to talk. Filmmakers can use this broody atmosphere to bring plot lines and developments to a head, to be played out in the taxi ride or afterwards.

Action movies of the 'follow that taxi' type use the vehicle in chases. Pursuing a criminal is a classic in taxi films, and these scenes can either be dramatic, entertaining, or comical. Often, the outcome is dependent on the script of the taxi driver.

The Taxi in Song

This chapter has shown that in many aspects of the socio-cultural world, be it graphic arts, TV, or film, taxis and taxi drivers and their cultural markers and identifiers have made a lasting impact. Somehow, the everyday life of the taxi world keeps inspiring the cultural world. Nowhere more so than in the realm of song, our last category. Although it is more difficult to pinpoint each taxi song inspired by the chequered band profession the world over, we've tried to list the major contributors. One thing which becomes immediately clear is how many bands there are who have called themselves 'taxi'. Even a rough search unearths hundreds of them in every part of the world.

In order to get his audience's impression of the most important taxi songs, The Guardian's Peter Kimpton in 2014 enlisted the help of his readers to make up a respectable list of cab-related songs (he modified the original list in 2018). Kimpton's intro to the story – splitting it in a taxi and a taxi driver-oriented piece – is priceless. In the first piece, he leans heavily on London-related knowledge; in the second one, the driver takes centre stage:

But more than transportation, a taxi represents a transaction based on mutual trust. More than simply A to B, a taxi is a brief moment in a hired capsule of privacy. It is the limousine of the elite and exclusive, it is the ticking meter clock of the city's official rate, it is the unlicensed and bargained, the Venetian water boat, the long-distance jitney, or it's the ramshackle hand-pulled, auto or cycle rickshaw.

With taxis and taxicabs being an indelible part of culture, it's no surprise then that taxi cabs have been staples of famous songs for years! Just like the drivers and passengers of taxi cabs, songs about taxis are hugely varied and stylistically different. Many are songs of love lost or new beginnings.

The Taxi in Transition

Not that the various cultural references have failed to keep up with the real politic of the industry. Gone are the cosy references to the 'mom and pop' town taxi, the singing driver, or any of the exaggerated character(s) typical in many portrayals. The singing and dancing were replaced by the gritty reality of the New York taxi market; the garage 'sparing pen' of the 1970s, or the vehicle as a backdrop for a sitcom, also faded over time. Even the whimsical relationships seen in the French taxi film franchise and set between Marseille Police and street-smart taxi driver portrayed in surreal style by Samy Naceri towards the end of the 1990s are moments that have passed, older pictures of an older industry. Replaced by the neurotic TNC driver Stu (Kumail Nanjiani) in 'Stuber' desperately looking for a five-star rating from his passengers. The TNC industry appearing alongside a cannon of gig economy reveals many displaying the desperation for top-class ratings, regardless of the possibility that average and topflight cannot be the same. Here then is a change in reference point from the garage-based taxi driver to the gig worker. A real-life change is reflected in the references of the media. The focus reflects the move to and increasing significance of individual ratings, the ability of the passenger to score their driver, and, less well known, the opposite as well. The media portrayal is an acceptance of, or at least an initial indication that, the five stars so desired by the gig driver are not simply niceties for a job well done but necessities to those relying on the platform for work. Film reflects reality here, whether exaggerated or maybe not so exaggerated after all!

Documentaries and 'infotainment' on the small screen have also moved on from the classic image of the taxi. Current exposes include the battles within the industry, while specific features, such as Super Pumped (Showtime), illustrate the battle for control within at larger TNCs and the ready conflicts of the gig industry as a whole. For its part, Uber supported the development of Spike Lee's "Da Republic of Brooklyn', a film focused on five drivers in New York's most populous borough, exposing the intricacies of working for the TNC.

Whether focused, presenting a point of view, observing, or critical, many of the traditional cultural references have changed. Caution must still be given to the snapshot as well as preconceived review but change of presentation as a reflection of a change in context can be significant and informative and is most definitely desirable.

4 Socio-economic and Political Theories

Having observed both the history and emergence of the present-day taxi and for hire industry, in this chapter, we consider the justification of theories pertaining to its regulation, role in transportation, and the relationship between the mode, its governance, and politics. We explore the structure of the market, its segments, and why these matter. We discuss whether its segmentation requires different regulations, including a review of the political and social pressures that influence this. We discuss the impacts of the entry of transportation network companies (TNCs) into the market, the impacts of lobbying and political pressures that the new technologies have brought, and the controversies that continue as the mode(s) continue to exist in different segments and different esteems.

We will, in the first instance, consider whether the definition of vehicles for hire represents a single market, albeit comprising various segments, or that of multiple and separate markets, related to or deserving of separate regulation. Equally, whether such regulations need to be strict, assuming a need to regulate, or light-touch, reliant on competitive market restraint as an alternative to the regulated competition. The chapter will also address the separation of for hire vehicle (FHV) regulations from those applicable to vehicle regulation on the whole, such as the need for a driving licence for any vehicle driver or the underlying need for all vehicles to be safe and the common practice of vehicle testing applied in most places to most vehicles.

For much of its history, the taxi market has been controlled by regulations, a form of market intervention most frequently argued as being in the public interest. An example of public interest controls can be seen in a regulator setting a rate of fares, also referred to as tariff. The intervention is argued in the public interest where a passenger has no reasonable way of knowing a rate of fare in advance of engagement, nor the opportunity to negotiate once engaged – the passenger has no way of knowing the quality or price of the service before the purchasing decision is made. In economic terms, these properties represent the first of a long series of market imperfections that may be visible in the taxi market and a logical justification for the regulation of that market.

DOI: 10.4324/9781003256311-5

Few industries have as clear a link between their existence and regulation as the taxi industry, while the regulations appear equally clear in their objective, if not their result. Taxi regulation is a combination of three areas of control, applied to the quantity, quality, and economic (QQE) aspects of operation. The presence of regulation places a burden on the regulator to maintain market-oriented operation, the approximation of market forces, where the market itself would fail to result in public benefits (market failure). This process is referred to as regulated competition, a different and generally incompatible mechanism when compared to the free-market competition, though it is equally important to note that all (legal) markets are subject to some forms of regulatory intervention, even where this is limited to the payment of tax or the certification of minimum standards.

This is not to say that all regulations are justified, with different segments (of the taxi industry) facing different challenges. Not all market segments suffer the same levels of imperfections, exampled by the different amounts of knowledge, e.g.: of fare, a passenger may obtain in advance of engaging a taxi in the pre-booked sector, compared to the hailed sector. This argument is also applicable to the engagement process where a TNC app is used to display a fare ahead of engagement, with most TNCs not facing regulatory control on most of their fares.[1]

Moreover, as the market comprises multiple relationships, between passenger and driver, driver and dispatcher, taxi company and regulator (amongst others), it is also subject to multiple layers of regulation.

FHV Market Segments

This section discusses market mechanisms visible in the different market segments of FHV transport as illustrated in Figure 4.1.

Here, we discuss the distinct characteristics of each, defining three primary and two additional segments, as being:

Primary Segments

- Hailed taxis (street hail), also known as cruising or street taxis, plying for hire and available for immediate engagement; this segment, together with stand taxis, can also be defined as a street segment.
- Stand taxis (ranking taxis) are those standing at taxi ranks and available on demand, normally on the basis of first in first out, though other models can exist. Taxi ranks are typically defined and controlled by a licensing authority and available for use to licensed vehicles, i.e. taxis. This segment, together with hailing, is a street segment. While most stands, aka ranks, are under the control of a street authority, leading to their definition as official ranks by some, a smaller number may be defined on private land, outwith the control of a highways agency or street authority. These 'private ranks' do not need to comply with regulatory requirements (in the main) and can define their own access requirements.

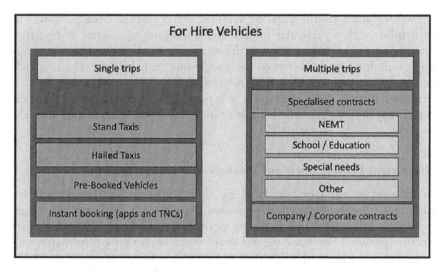

Figure 4.1 Common split of vehicle category by use.

Examples of private ranks include those at supermarkets, within private ground, at hotels, airports, etc.

- Pre-booked vehicles include those dispatched by a taxi company, broker, or radio circuit. This category also includes TNCs in the UK, though it is more common for TNCs to be categorised separately and in isolation, particularly in North American markets.

Additional segments

- TNCs are also known by a variety of alternative terms, including corporate brand names. The segment bears many similarities to the traditional pre-booked segment but may reflect a number of variations around price, testing, and driver registration requirements.
- Contract hire is a sub-categorisation of the pre-booked taxi market. Private contracts can include, but need not be limited to, non-emergency medical transport (NEMT), schools/education transport, corporate transport, and similar.

The major change that has occurred since the introduction of TNCs has been a change in the relative importance of the market segments illustrated above. The hailed market is generally observed to be in decline, while pre-booked vehicles, including TNCs, are increasing in market share. This does not mean, however, that street hailing has disappeared. Neither have app bookings solved all of the taxi market's economic challenges, but rather that a shift in engagement methods has impacted the viability of some market participants and advantaged others.

Looking at the relationships between the driver and the customer can also be helpful, with a particular impact of sub-division to a series of partially interlinked market segments with different economic properties. The most important distinction is between street segments, including street hailing and taxi ranks, on the one side, and pre-booking/dispatch, on the other. By focusing on private, single-trip travel, it is possible to present different theories explaining the mechanisms that justify different forms of regulation in each segment.

Distinctions Between Street and Pre-booked Dispatch Segments

In this context, the term 'pre-booking' means any booking through a third party (*UK: Booking Office; Canada: Broker; US: Dispatch*). Bookings can range from near-immediate service (asap) to ordering in advance. The key distinction between pre-booking and street segments is that a third party, i.e. a dispatcher (including hailing apps and TNCs), is involved (see Figure 4.2). For pre-booked trips, various actors are involved, including taxis, private hire vehicles (PHVs), minicabs, and limousines depending on locational and regulatory contexts.

In the following section, we focus on the link between economic mechanisms in these segments and issues that call for regulatory intervention or non-intervention, such as public safety and security, fair treatment of passengers with respect to quality and price, environmental concerns, congestion, working conditions, city image, and competition. These issues have all been affected by TNC services and will be affected by the commercial

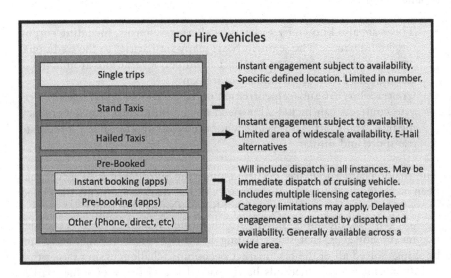

Figure 4.2 Distinctions between single-trip categorisations.

arrival of automated and autonomous vehicles operating on-demand services in fleets.

Street Segments

Street segments, including street hailing and ranking markets, are long established and will often pre-date motorisation, the stand providing additional certainty to driver and passenger alike, cruising, increasing the geographical distribution, again in the favour of both passenger and driver.

Traditionally, cruising cabs operate by 'plying for hire', driving around empty looking for passengers. The model is effective where large numbers of passengers may be seeking taxis, typically in metropolitan city centres or other locations of high-density demand, making the model viable to vehicles wishing to supply transport services in city centres. An intending passenger engages a vehicle by hailing as a taxi passes. Most cities require cruising taxis to display externally mounted signs, aka taxi roof domes, indicating availability, often using vacant sign or light, though the exact pattern will differ by location. If the taxi density (supply) is too low, it will not be worthwhile waiting for a taxi to pass by. If the number of passengers is too low, active cruising to try to find passengers will not be economical, as the act of cruising itself comes with a cost to the driver.

The economics of the cruising and stand segments are widely reported in academic literature, both theoretically and empirically. The literature broadly reaches consensus that this market segment can suffer market failure that needs to be corrected by policy in order to function optimally. The main reason for this is that when the taxi and customer meet, the customer is faced with a temporary monopoly supplier (Dempsey, 1996). For the potential passenger, choosing to wait, i.e. not engaging the first taxi, means uncertainty. He or she does not know when the next vacant taxi will pass by, nor, in an unregulated market, what fare would be charged. This uncertainty gives bargaining power to the taxi driver, putting the passenger at a disadvantage and contributing to a lack of price competition at the point of use in this market segment.

If prices are not set by regulation and can be set by the supplier at the time of use, any incentive to discount is lost and may be replaced by profit maximising behaviour on the part of the driver, effectively creating unpredictable pricing that may become monopolistic in nature. There is no continuous supply or demand function that would otherwise result in equilibrium pricing, giving rise to the concept of instant monopolies and monopolistic abuse. It can also be suggested that there are little or no economies of scale for a cruising taxi, as the market is transient and has no shelf life beyond the willingness of a passenger to wait for the next vehicle.

The market requires a minimum fleet and customer density, at system level, to function, making the mode an effective option against other travel choices, but when that is in place, only small benefits result from cooperation and coordination within the supply side. Coordination as can be seen is more likely to reflect corporate level, or associations, as effective bargaining tools in response to regulation of fares, etc., with none at the individual driver level or at the point of use.

Many cities find, or have at a point in history found, the free-market solution for the street market segments is unattractive and have imposed regulations. These regulations can take different forms that may typically include minimum vehicle standards: uniformed vehicles, taximeters, and identifiable driver IDs (quality control) and other forms of regulation. The perception and/or reality of oversupply has been tackled by constraints on the number of vehicles and/or licensed drivers (quantity constraint) and may include medallion systems, such as those applied in New York, where the licence is transferable and maintains a value in its own right. The New York medallion system is widely quoted, not least because of high medallion values. Other similar regulations include restricting the type of vehicle as the case with black taxis in London (hackney carriages) or requiring the drivers to have minimum qualifications, as exampled by the taxi 'knowledge', a local operating test required of drivers in London, amongst other cities. Fares can also be set at a local licensing authority level, whether by diktat or in agreement between the authority and an association of licensed taxi drivers/owners. The resulting tariff has the effect of not only preventing (reducing[2]) monopolistic abuses of price but also limiting the possibilities for dynamic pricing and reducing incentives for price competition.

Controls may also be applied to infrastructure, including taxi ranks (Scot.: stands/US: lines). Public stands are under the control of an authority, which can determine location, size, operating hours, etc., and are typically found at transport hubs such as airports, railway stations, hotels, and significant city locations. Not all stands are under the control of the local licensing or highway authority, with a number, of private stands, under the control of a private organisation, shop, or hotel, though these are unlikely to be located directly on a public highway. A common practice has developed over time in relation to taxi stand etiquette, with many organised on the basis of first (vehicle) in first out. Even when this is not the case, there is a strong tendency for people to choose the first taxi in the rank, a practice that further restricts price competition at the point of use.

From an economic perspective, the rank has many of the same properties as the cruising market segments but does not rely on the same level of market density as for hailing. Engagement occurs at a defined location – the taxi rank, rather than being spread over a wider road network, resulting in fewer 'dead kilometres', the distance travelled without a passenger, and has a higher likelihood of engagement, for both the driver and passenger once at the rank.

As in the case of the cruising segment, in the absence of economic regulation, free-market pressures may result in an upward pressure on fares, as customers are faced with a monopoly supplier in most cases. While it may be arguable that some price competition may exist, for example between taxis from different companies, observational evidence suggests a very strong social norm towards passengers moving to the first vehicle in the line, reducing the opportunity for price comparison. Or where conditions may allow for some price competition, little incentive exists for drivers to offer lower fares to increase demand, with a reverse incentive for drivers to maximise income through the reinforcement of the first in first out principle.

There are few, if any, economies of scale in the taxi market. In an unregulated market, this will result in a high number of vehicles, low wages, and low or unpredictable profits and may create incentives to reduce quality. As a result, an open-/free-market solution is found not to be attractive in many cities. This market segment is often regulated. Typical regulations include licensing (you need a licence in order to drive legally), restricting entry (cap on number of licences, unmet demand test, etc.), quality requirements for drivers (local knowledge, language, etc.) and vehicles (technical specifications, accessibility, etc.), and regulated prices (and/or price information).

Pre-booked/Dispatch Market Segments

The practice of pre-booking a vehicle is a more recent innovation than cruising or stand markets. The market is dependent on suitable information and communications technologies (ICTs) and has grown as the quality and availability of ICTs have improved. The pre-booked sector will often follow technological innovation, exampled by an increase in use as (landline) telephones became widespread, with further increases observed in line with the launch and uptake of two-way radios, which improved the quality and reliability of services that could be offered and more recently by digital booking systems. Radio and digital systems supported the development of in-vehicle equipment, receivers, and digital displays, each adding an element of reliability and utility, culminating in the current generation of app systems. Apps appear to be the most commonly used form of pre-booking in use at the time of writing.

From an economic point of view, the pre-booked market is very different from cruising and stand markets. The nature of pre-booking has changed the relationships between passenger and driver and introduced a third party – a dispatcher or a TNC – with the role of mediating the trip. Dispatch can include either or both a staffed office and/or computerised systems. Some authorities require the physical presence of the dispatch function within its area, though this is likely to decline as the nature of the technology moves from physical to virtual and remote, while dispatch companies themselves can see savings in adopting automated and computerised processes.

The dispatch market segment differs from the cruising and stand markets, as there can be significant economies of scale on the supply side. Economies of density can also be seen, meaning that the more vehicles available through a booking platform the more attractive that platform is. Economies of scale are also likely, where the purchase and maintenance of the ICT system is spread across a larger number of vehicles, making larger regional, national, or cloud systems more cost effective to the operator.

It has been suggested that the ICT systems are relatively expensive compared to the much lower technology costs of the street segment, but it is also appropriate to note that the investment costs are spread across multiple vehicles. It is also likely that a number of street operators will avoid joining a dispatch service, as many currently charge the driver subscriptions or per-trip fees that would be avoided by driving as a 'street taxi' only.

Other cost elements may also differ from the street market, including where the passenger can benefit from a better bargaining situation, at least in theory. The passenger is able to identify and compare different companies for price and availability, though it remains unlikely that negotiation at the point of use would occur. It may also be easier for the passenger to build up a set of experiences with different companies, identifying the best company for them, giving rise to potential brand loyalties and repeat business, both significantly less likely in the street sector. The presence of repeat customers creates an incentive for competition, whether on price or quality, that would not exist in the cruising market.

As a result, the pre-booked market can function quite well with much less regulation than its street equivalents. This said, most locations continue to apply some forms of regulation on the segment. Typical controls apply to quality requirements (on vehicles and drivers) to ensure safety, and non-discrimination, and requirements on opening hours, to ensure availability. Also, the double economies of scale involved, both relating to density and fixed costs, points towards local, regional, or even global monopolies as a real possibility, even with limited barriers to entry.

Contracted Segments

Contracted segments can refer to public service transport, such as schools or NEMT uses, and to exclusive corporate transport under contract.

In many cases, public authorities and private companies have a recurring need for taxi services. For the public authority, this may be in the form of transport of schoolchildren, elderly, disabled, and so on. For private companies, it may be to transport personnel on a regular or semi-regular basis. In both cases, taxi services can be an economically attractive alternative to producing such services in-house. In these market segments, the taxi industry will normally face competition from other industries, depending upon the legal framework. In the same way, as with the pre-booked market segments, this segment can function quite well with little regulation (Table 4.1).

Regulatory Approaches – QQE

As shown in other chapters in this book, regulation has a long history. Some of the regulations in force are best understood through their historical context,

Table 4.1 Optimal regulation by market segment

	Street segments		Booked segments	
	Cruising	Stand	Pre-booked segment	Contract segment
Challenges that may call for regulation	Maintaining quality of service; maintaining efficient prices, roadworthy vehicles, and qualified drivers.		Market forces should keep supply, quality, and price efficient. Maintaining competition is a major issue, due to network economies. Balancing economies of scale against benefits from competition, preventing monopolies.	
Theoretical solution	Regulated price, quality regulations, and (for social reasons, i.e. congestion and operator economy) quantity restrictions may be called for. However, quantity can also be regulated through quality or economic regulation.		Subsidised monopoly can maximise social welfare. Market solutions should be efficient. Regulation on externalities.	Market solution regarding price, supply, and quality.

reflecting different market control motivations at the time of first regulation. We would also argue a political context to some areas of regulation, reflecting customer, industry, and political imperatives at the time of regulation, and its, various, reforms.

From an economic perspective, regulation can often follow market failure, in particular a lack of information (regarding price, quality, and availability) in the street market segments, cruising and stand, often related to the interaction between the driver and the customer. Another important relationship, and subsequent regulation, relates to the interaction between the driver and the authorities. However, it is the control and limitation on market entry that has received the most attention. The subject is frequently reported in both public and academic debate and is most controversial when applied in the form of a cap on licence numbers.

Taxi regulation will most frequently fall under one of three headings, QQE control, related to:

- Quality regulations typically address the operator's fitness for operation, standards of vehicle, insurance, driver knowledge, etc.
- Quantity regulations will address the number of vehicles available.
- Economic regulation will typically relate to the fares and fees.

Having defined the primary areas of regulation, it is also important to highlight notable exceptions. Airports constitute a special case and may differ from the regulatory controls common and outlined above, both in their definition and application. Differences experienced at airports frequently stem from one of two primary concerns. The first being that larger airports can, and frequently do, sit outside the administrative authority of the city (cities) they serve. Thus, Glasgow International Airport is physically located in the authority area of Renfrewshire. More extreme examples also exist, including Basel airport, Switzerland, which actually sits in the territorial area of France, with exits into both countries, though these are an exception, rather than a rule. The second critical issue being the market for taxi transport at airports can differ significantly from the needs of the city. The airport is also the first encounter travellers have with a new city. The latter fact increases the information asymmetry issues. Travellers often do not have extensive knowledge of the city they arrive at. They may not know the best way of reaching their destination, nor how much such a trip should cost. Airport authorities will frequently adopt their own regulations, sometimes at odds with the cities they serve. In the following subsections, we will introduce and explain the rationale for primary areas of controls and the differences in 'exceptional' and specific circumstances.

Quality Regulation

Quality regulation refers to controls applied to standards of service offered. There are arguments for different forms of qualitative regulations, usually these are combined in a series of criteria that are required to get a licence. Quality regulations may be applied to the driver, the vehicle, and/or the operating company and can include a mix of measured and judged standards, including vehicle fitness, driver knowledge, and/or fit and proper person checks, including of the operating company.

Controls may require testing and certification that can be carried out by an authority, its agency, or approved certification body, which need not be a public authority. In the case of many TNCs, the company itself may *de facto* regulate the quality and standards both of their drivers and vehicles.

The primary argument for licensing is to ensure public safety by only allowing qualified vehicles and drivers access to the taxi markets. Licences can be set up in a number of ways, depending on local regulation. Licences for vehicles may require that the vehicles meet certain technical standards, such as meeting certain safety requirements and being instantly recognisable as a taxi. This can also include details on livery and type of vehicle. An example of vehicle type regulation includes the Metropolitan Conditions of Fitness (MCF), a vehicle standard developed in London in 1906, and most recently updated in 2019,[3] that defines vehicle performance specifications for licensed taxis. The MCF has been adopted in a number of larger cities in the UK and has included strict requirements for vehicle performance, including a stringent turning circle requirement that has excluded a number of potential taxi vehicle types from the market.

The assurance of safety is generally accepted as a minimum requirement, both insofar as the vehicle should be roadworthy and drivers vetted, typically through a criminal background check. Other requirements such as livery and vehicle type requirements are more ambiguous. This does not mean that such requirements always are out of place. It can be argued that such requirements are justified, as they are part of the city or brand experience. They can also help to prevent fraud: illegal operators can be easier to spot and so on. Standardised vehicle appearances were applied to the Washington DC taxi fleet from 2013, adopting an all-over red design, known locally as the 'taxi uniform' or 'uniform color' and justified as matching other District of Columbia transit color schemes, notably the city's new streetcar services and that of the district supported DC circulator bus.

Recognisable and common colours also appear within taxi companies, including in locations where a separate and defined 'color scheme' is a requirement of each operator. Cities where distinct company-specific 'color schemes' are required include Seattle, WA and Los Angeles, CA, amongst others.

In other cities, including London, Glasgow, and Edinburgh, common aspects of vehicle appearance result from standard vehicle type specifications applied in those cities (the MCF), resulting in a limited number of vehicle types being able to enter service and high concentrations of a single vehicle type in the fleet.

A uniform vehicle livery can also result in ready identification as to which vehicles are taxis, including the selection of a company where each displays

Image 4.1 New York City color scheme applied to Toyota Prius.
Source: Authors.

Image 4.2 'London taxi' shown in service in Glasgow. Designed to meet Conditions
   of Fitness Standards.
Source: Authors.

its own livery but may also limit the possibility of service differentiation,
where each taxi will (should) offer the same service at the same price. The
term 'livery' is also being adopted in some US commentaries as a description
of the limousine/private hire sector.

Licensing drivers can also mean many things. Typical safety requirements
include the need to have a valid driver's licence, a near universal requirement for all drivers, and a clean criminal record. In addition, a documented
knowledge of the local area may be called for. To what extent is debated, in
particular after the common access to satellite navigation. Knowledge of the
local language, and in cases where this is a minor language, and knowledge of
an international language can be considered necessary. A lesser requirement
where much of the transaction can occur digitally, e.g. via an app.

The exact definition of qualitative requirements will influence the outcome of the system. Strict qualitative requirements on drivers may act as a
strong barrier to market entry and up-scaling for TNCs. The absence of, or
lenient, enforcement of such requirements may result in lower service levels;
and the combination of control and enforcement will impact on the overall
perception of service level.

The licensing of the dispatch function can also add another dimension to
markers delivery. Economies of scale can exist in the dispatch of services,

including those via apps, while some may be seen as 'natural monopolies' (Arnott, 1996), particularly in smaller markets. It can also be argued that licensing of TNCs/dispatchers may allow a delegation of the administrative burden of licensing vehicles and drivers to these companies, particularly in terms of record keeping and some elements of driver checking. A downside to this is related to the potential the information asymmetries associated with such a delegation of power and the potential private economic rent that can be extracted from market dominance in the pre-booking segments.

Quantity Regulation

Quantity regulations, limiting the number of licences, have a long history in the taxi/VHF markets and relate to the right to operate, legally, whether as a licensed vehicle, driver, or both. Licences can be named after their physical representations, the Medallion in New York; Decal, elsewhere in the USA; or Taxi Plate, UK; or by other similar terms. Licences may be 'owned', as property, in some locations – by a driver, company, broker, etc., implying an asset value to that licence that is separate from its administrative cost; or be retained by the authority, non-transferable, often required to be handed back on exit from the industry. In some locations, licences are transferable in given circumstances alone, for example where kept within a family, passed on to children, or associated with a company where that company, rather than the licence, is bought and sold (inclusive of licence).

Much has been made of the excess transfer values of the medallion, including the peak in values of the New York plates at around $1.5 million per medallion at its highest. Transferable 'owned' medallions have also spawned a medallion loan industry, particularly in the USA, with banking and loan companies focused entirely on funding the purchase of the medallion. The added costs, of the medallion and its loan payment costs, weigh the industry as a burden, often without significant benefit, and create issues in the balance of cost to income and eventually on fares.

Even where licences are distributed without cost, beyond their administrative cost, where issued for vehicles and drivers, the question remains as to how such licences are distributed. Two main approaches can be observed: one a limitation on the number of licences issued by whom, to whom, and at what frequency/justification; the other allowing all qualified to enter, with what qualification, issued by whom? However, even this distinction need not be clear-cut. Examples exist of nominally capped markets, such as the case in many Norwegian counties pre-2020, where the number of awarded licences was larger than the number of vehicles in use, while a series of arguments have followed from TNC introduction as to the 'competent' authority appropriate to test or approve either vehicle or driver. Furthermore, the introduction of red tape, even in open markets, can create a barrier to entry. The market outcome will be determined by how each of these solutions is implemented.

There are several rationales used for limiting entry into the taxi market. One is to prevent crowding at stands or in city centres; the second is to maintain profitability amongst operators (to compensate for other duties, such as a 24-hour service requirement or specific quality standards); the third is to protect workers, as one typically finds lower wages and longer working hours for the drivers in open entry system. The main arguments against entry regulation are: (1) that entry regulation creates economic rent and (2) that such restrictions are not a market solution.

Economic Regulation

Economic orthodoxy suggests prices will fall if excess capacity is introduced into a market. The effect follows from market pressures around equilibrium, if a price falls, more of the good/service is consumed, and its corollary, the greater the level of supply the more downward pressure on price exists. Paradoxically, the opposite is often observed in the taxi industry (Dempsey, 1996; Bekken and Longva, 2003), particularly in street market segments (hail and rank). Excess supply creates the economic incentives for an individual taxi owner, company, or driver to increase fares, where permitted to do so. This is a result of a series of market imperfections. One of these imperfections is that competitive shopping is impractical; it can induce significant transaction costs in the hail and rank market segments. As noted by Shreiber (1975), an individual cab operator, acting independently, cannot gain more passengers if he alone reduces his price below the going market rate. However, Shreiber (ibid.) also notes that there is elasticity between taxi and other public transport modes. As a result, the upward pressure on the price from the individual taxi driver may lead to a lower market share for the taxi industry than in a market with fixed or maximum fares.

A practical solution to this problem may be the application of controls to the level of fare that may be charged, usually in the form of a tariff, by stating the maximum price the taxis are allowed to charge, at least in the hail and rank market segments. That means that if the market price is below the regulated price, the market price can be used; if it is above the regulated price, the regulated price will be used. It is, however, very difficult to set a 'correct' regulated price. The taxi industry will usually lobby for a higher fare, while members of the public, their elected representatives, and often the press, will typically seek a lower fare. A series of defined approaches have emerged, often associated with a taxi cost or industrial price index, but even the presence of a measured or modelled approach is typically unlikely to prevent interest groups or avoid appeal.

A regulated maximum fare can also help protect the public from arbitrarily higher fares charged by opportunistic taxi drivers, for whom each trip is typically treated in isolation; it is being unlikely that the same driver would encounter the same passenger again, and that if the passenger complains, he or she will not be able to identify the driver in question. However, it being set as a maximum, rather than an exact fare, would still allow a driver or company to give discounts if the market fare is below the regulated fare. This said, it remains questionable whether drivers would, at the point of use, choose to offer a fare other than the defined maximum.

In the pre-booked market segments, it is more difficult to find a good economic argument for price caps. The segment offers a greater potential for competition compared to the hailed sector, except in the cases where the taxi industry is organised as a monopoly. Also, in such cases, there will, most likely, still be a form of intermodal competition, creating cross-elastic limits to taxi fare levels. Only in the case where the taxi service is a true monopoly, that is if it is the only viable public transport option (this can be the case in rural areas or niche market segments), one would expect a pre-booked service to charge monopoly prices. Even in these cases, the requirement for retaining such a pricing policy will be the requirement to maintain the taxi company's role as a monopoly supplier.

Airport Regulation

While the fundamentals of taxi regulation do not alter from those described above, that the QQE principles remain the same, the context and needs of an airport can be significantly different. Priorities for the airport authority are focused on a specific series of vehicle uses, including the ability of the airport taxi fleet to provide services to customers without significant delay: that sufficient information is provided and that the ground transport experience be consistent with the image of the airport itself.

For the taxi driver, potential passengers flying into the airport can represent a demand that has low market awareness and low price sensitivity. The passenger is less likely to have a complex understanding of their environment and of taxi service standards. An uncontrolled market might make for high fares, placing a burden on the supplier to take a responsible stand and for the (airport) regulator a responsibility to regulate appropriately.

As many airports will typically control the land they are located on, their taxi services can be regulated specifically to their needs. Controls will frequently seek to ensure large fleets are available at short notice and will sometimes be supported by large, on airfield, holding areas and driver resting facilities. While drivers can wait extended periods without passengers, the carriage of a passenger is often more lucrative than cruising within the city. Competition between airports will support this effort; as the taxi is typically a first and last view of the airport, and of the city, tighter regulations can be applied than elsewhere.

In order to avoid congestion, FHVs are typically held at a depot some distance away from the terminal they serve. This allows physical separation of the uninformed passenger from the informed drivers. Automated systems or manual dispatchers can call in vehicles at request, opening opportunities for efficient traffic management and quality control. On the negative side, long waits and high fees at airports also may create a set of issues related to unserved areas and drivers rejecting short trips.

As the market for taxis has been expanded to include TNC provision, so many airports have been obliged to take account of the new service types. As TNCs retain some of the controls previously adopted by the airport, namely fare and dispatch functions, so the pressure to adapt to new operating practices has emerged. Innovations have followed, including the concept of a taxi rank-oriented TNC system, effectively a first-up system for TNCs, with alternatives based on coloured and numbered identifiers sometimes referred to as PINs or visible through the use of coloured beacons.

The example of Gardermoen airport, which serves Oslo, provides an illustration of some of these factors. The airport is located approximately 50 km from downtown Oslo and is mainly served by train and bus services. The airport also generates a large number of taxi trips (Denstadli et al., 2012; Thune-Larsen and Farstad, 2018). In 2019, 14 taxi companies served the airport. Access to the airport was organised by a separate company 'Taxi Depot AS', who managed the taxi ranks and holding area for taxis. The holding area was located approximately 500 meters from the terminal. At the terminal, there was a taxi rank management officer, and an information service, offering both automated and manual price and availability information. At the rank, the spots closest to the exit were used for taxis requested by passengers, while a handful of spots were allocated to the taxis that had waited the longest at the depot.

As price information was readily available, and the passengers were free to choose the taxi company of their preference, one would expect prices to converge and in general be 'reasonable'; however, this was not the case. At random day tests, the price charged by the most expensive taxi company was 2.7 times as high as that.

A different experience can be illustrated by Charlotte Douglas International Airport in North Carolina. The airport serves the metro area of Charlotte and is some 18 km west of the city. The airport is owned by the city authority, Mecklenburg County. The airport defines its own regulatory standards and permits operation by four airport taxi companies, which will also operate in the city.

The airport has invested in facilities for both taxi and TNC operators, while defining strict standards on vehicle type, availability, and service standards. Taxi fares are also controlled, while TNC fares are set by the TNC. The airport utilises an automated call forward for vehicles between a joint holding lot and the arrivals curbside. As taxi fares are controlled, there are no differentials by operator.

Impact of TNCs on Taxi Market Segments and Their Regulation

The major change that has occurred in the vehicle for hire market, predicating a rebalancing between FHVs, and across the wider market for transport, has been the emergence and large-scale introduction of TNCs. In this subsection, we look at how these change the relations which are relevant for regulation. To do so, we need to place TNCs in the context of societal change. The change created, or at least facilitated by, digitalisation, and specifically the emergence of smartphones. In this description, the term digitalisation is used to refer to the broad set of changes allowed by the implementation of ICTs.

From the economic standpoint, the digital technologies can result in *'lower search costs, lower replication cost, lower transportation cost, lower tracking cost and lower verification costs'* in the taxi market (Goldfarb and Tucker, 2019). All of these impact on the competitive nature of the market. Lower search costs mean that it becomes possible to alleviate one of the major issues that has been the cause of market failures in the cruising market segments – that the customer does not know when the next vehicle is likely to be available. Now, the information is searchable via an app with a high degree of accuracy. Lower replication costs influence the cost of providing a booking in much the same way. The booking process can be streamlined and digitised, where this functionality is included. Cash can be removed from the system, reducing the transaction costs and increasing relative security, while lower operational costs are achieved with the move of booking functions from a physical medium to a digital one.

Lower tracking costs may result and relate to: navigation, the investment in route knowledge, reducing the skill set needed to operate a taxi vehicle; lower verification costs, that the quality is recorded via a series of review processes, both of driver and passenger; and third-party verification of identities. The mutual verification of drivers and customers reduces the driver's risk of facing customers who do not pay or do not behave and the customer's risk of encountering unskilled or unsafe drivers.

TNCs also introduce organisational forms that scale better than their traditional counterparts. Although there has been a long history within the traditional industry of IT system development, most IT companies had not targeted individual owners, as might the TNC platform, concentrating rather on the existing dispatch structures. The arrival of TNCs and the emerging digital platforms changed the nature of the dispatch technologies (Kenney and Zysman, 2016), the new entrants functioning as two-sided markets (Rochet and Tirole, 2003), in which the producers buy into a market network of potential customers, and the customers buy access to a large set of potential service providers. The platform provides introduction, verification, and transaction services in order to facilitate the operation not necessary in, or part of, the traditional dispatch system. This change in emphasis has allowed the emerging platforms to better match supply with demand through pricing than possible in earlier dispatch systems. The TNC platforms are observed to apply both lower, and higher fares as a result of the technologies, with surge pricing, the application of fare multipliers (including some very significant up-charges, when demand is high and supply is low; and the potential for subsidised trips when demand is low and supply high. It is also possible to subsidise one side of the market over an extended period of time in order to better match supply with demand.

The regulatory implication of this can be seen against three metrics. First, the new systems solve a number of the traditional taxi market failures. Second, it creates new issues relating to competition at different economic scales than what has previously been the case. Third, it creates new challenges that call for regulation.

1   Solving market failures typically result in more efficient market operation. This means that more transactions take place and utility is higher. This effect is well documented in the literature (Rayle et al., 2016), etc. This effect should increase the market share of trips booked through TNC, both in absolute and relative numbers.

2   The different scales of operation between traditional taxi operators and TNCs are challenging. For the authorities, it means that the relevant scope of the market shifted from city level to a regional, national, or even global level for the connecting part of the service, while operation is still local.

      This can create situations where different tiers of government have conflicting interests. This again points towards new market failures (local monopolies, or situations with over- or undersupply) and regulatory entrepreneurship. The latter is where the TNCs utilise the dissonance between different tiers of government in order to create loopholes and avoid unwanted regulations, or use their skill and political power to create a new set of regulations that better suits their operation (Pelzer et al., 2019).

      The scale of operation of TNCs also shifts the power relation between the operating company and the regulatory authority. Before the TNCs, local authorities often had more access to resources (expertise, lawyers) than the local operating companies, while this has changed with multi-national TNCs.

3   TNCs have created new challenges in terms of the club good nature of the service, persons without digital competence, banking, or other entry criteria are effectively excluded from the service. And there are issues related to labour in a market dominated by digital platforms (c.f. the platform-dependent entrepreneur literature [Cutolo and Kenney, 2019; Oppegaard, 2021]).

Possible Regulatory Approaches to Address the New Challenges

The extent to which the FHV market can remain subject to regulation is unclear. The rebalancing between market segments, though well established, is not finished, with emergence from the Covid pandemic creating new challenges in and of itself. Public and political attitudes have changed over time, with the form and structure of the market contributing to an unease and mismatch between earlier regulations and those emerging with the new mode. Equally, it is visible that the TNCs have contributed to their own challenges, as the new, TNC, segment has catalysed new demand and high level of user uptake. By reducing disutility that may have been traditionally associated with taxi travel, the new entrant vehicles have become available to more people, supporting an increase in supply. This increases the welfare of both passengers and drivers, ceteris paribus, but is not entirely unproblematic as FHVs contribute to pollution and congestion in most cities (International Transport Forum, 2020). From the city perspective, space is a scarce commodity and energy use from mobility is something to be minimised. This means that increasing the market share of FHVs is only attractive to the extent that it reduces private vehicle use, Pareto optimisation, and this effect is not well documented. Studies typically find an unclear relation (Bekka et al., 2020) or that TNCs increase congestion (Schaller, 2017).

In this case, the main negative externality is vehicle kilometres produced without passengers, either through oversupply or inefficiency. Both issues can be addressed by 'smart' regulations, such as taxing empty vehicle kilometres. Structural regulations may follow, as a result of the emerging technologies; examples including vehicle controls, only allowing efficient TNCs to operate; or more basic controls, including on quantity, limiting the number of vehicles allowed on the roads.

For the 'smart' regulations to work, it will require an extensive data collection/sharing system to be in place. While it is true that the new systems create and maintain comprehensive datasets on operation, the willingness to share this information appears limited amongst the new commercial operators, particularly where such largess would be likely to result in higher levels of regulation and cost. Such a system would also need to work across different operators equally in the same area and may face issues of equity and the practice of 'multi-homing', where a driver is connected to more than one TNC at the same time or during the day. It should also include taxes on the negative externalities the city wishes to target.

In the case of changing scales of operation, the challenges presented by TNCs are shared with other multi-national companies, in that their operations are difficult to map and tax. Super-national framework regulations, giving clear divisions of responsibility, might be a way forward; for such regulations to work according to intentions, they need to provide equal treatment for equal service and allow local externalities to be regulated at the local level.

In many ways, TNCs can be seen as what in economic terms can be called club goods. These are services that are non–rivalrous and excludable. That is to say that a user's benefit from the good, being connected to a TNC, either from a passenger or driver side, is not decreasing other users' benefit but, on the contrary, there are economic benefits from having a larger user base. This can be either by users being required to have a credit card, a new smartphone, or fully functioning limbs in order to travel. This excludability creates issues as they may well result in the less privileged paying a higher price for a lower level of service than the ones that are able to access the club good. The club good nature also creates lock-in effects, limiting competition between TNCs.

Further Regulatory Issues

Labour Supply

A number of labour market effects are observable and some unique to the FHV industry. The industry can be seen as having low or limited barriers to entry, and it can be observed to comprise short-term workers, students, and early career drivers, a facet made more common by new entrants and a reliance, by some, on a rapid turnover in staff. The industry can also face specific earnings expectation behaviour, including the concept of driver income 'satisficing', seeking only to reach a pre-determined level of income, also known as 'reference-earnings', and then stops when that target is reached. This creates an inverse supply curve. The extent and effect of this practice is explored (Camerer et al., 1997; Agarwal et al., 2015; Farber, 2015) with mixed empirical results. Interviews point in the direction that the reference earnings approach is a real issue, in that drivers use reference earnings in their daily decisions on labour supply. However, that other factors, such as predefined shift patterns, can limit the behaviour but not prevent it.

Another reoccurring labour issue is the inverse labour supply model. In short, stating that when the economy is going well and there is a lot of demand for taxi services, the supply of skilled drivers is low, as they find other and better-paying employment in other sectors, and that in times of low demand, the supply is high. This may be a result of business cycles, where the taxi industry may function as an employer of last resort. This argument has anecdotal validity and some clear historical cases, related to the Great Depression, but with parallels in the financial crisis of 2008, and more recently, in the Covid pandemic. Still, it might not be a good explanation for labour supply in high-income countries in an age of migration and a context of limited supply of high-paying jobs with limited formal skills requirements.

Network Economics

Studies on the economies of scale of the taxi industry typically find that there are very limited if any benefits to scale in vehicle operations. Significant economies of scale are more likely in vehicle coordination and dispatch. Based on an observation of these economies of scale from vehicle densities and in parallel to Mohring (1972), Arnott (1996) argues that taxi travel should be subsidised in a first best solution.

The issue with economies of scale in a service that has a clear geographical scope is that it points towards local or regional market dominance. In any given area, the actor with the largest network of either drivers or customers will be able to offer better deals to the other side than the smaller competitors. These benefits of scale are, on the one hand, highly desirable, as they allow the system to be more efficient. On the other hand, they are highly undesirable as it increases the cost of market entry. And creates the possibility for a dominant actor to leverage the market position and create a *de facto* market position as a monopsonist of supply and monopolist in demand, although it is argued that market dominance is difficult to achieve in two-sided markets (Rochet and Tirole, 2003).

Political Economics

There is some evidence that the regulation of taxis has followed a regulatory cycle, drawing on the work by Needham (1983) who argues that regulation is a dynamic process that operates in a world of uncertainty, with multiple and conflicting interests. As a result, the outcome of a regulation does not always align with the intentions behind the regulation.

In mobility, this concept has been used to study bus regulation by Gwilliam (2008), who argues that bus regulation moves from a regulated public monopoly to a situation of competitive private supply, then to a private sector area monopoly, which evolves to a regulated private monopoly and then back to a regulated public monopoly. This framework may also have some relevance for FHV. As Dempsey (1996) points at the developments in American taxicab regulation, stating that American cities began regulating local taxi firms in the 1920s. From the 1970s, more than 20 cities (his sample) totally or partially deregulated their taxi companies. Furthermore, he states that the experience with taxicab deregulation was so profoundly unsatisfactory that virtually every city that embraced deregulation has since resumed economic regulation, despite strong deregulation ideology. This cycle predates the current developments in regulation with deregulation following the introduction of TNC services and various attempts to re-regulate following negative externalities from these services.

The deregulation following the introduction of TNCs is different from this regulatory cycle process, in that deregulation of the existing industries or re-regulation along different paths is linked directly with services that are introduced as 'new'. This can be seen as part of a legitimation work, with the aim of creating regime change in line with Lawrence and Suddaby (2006) and Fuenfschilling and Truffer (2016). These studies point at the different forms of institutional work associated with the establishment of a new regime, as opposed to the regulatory cycle framework which represents regime change, in that the actors represented remain stable over time, but their relations change. These points can be adopted to how TNCs have acted in the FHV sector.

Table 4.2 presents a framework used for analysing how institutional alignment and over time legitimacy can be actively constructed. Some of these actions are based on delegitimising existing structures while others are focused on creating new and alternative institutions. Although the framework has been developed in a different setting, the components seem parallel to

Table 4.2 Legitimation work for introducing TNCs

Form of work	Meaning	Examples
Advocacy	Mobilising support through a direct deliberate social suasion	Convincing politicians, the public, and investors of the need for TNCs by lobbying, meetings, marketing, etc.
Defining	Constructing a rule system that differs from the pre-existing rules and establishing new hierarchies	Presenting TNCs as something qualitatively different from pre-existing actors.
Vesting	Creating rule structures that confer property rights	Creating loyalty through handing out shares and conditioned investment (in vehicles).
Constructing new identities	Constructing new identities by redefining the relationship between actors and the field they operate in	Relabelling workers as partners.
Changing normative associations	Re-making the connections between previously established practices	Re-interpreting existing practices from alternative normative perspectives, such as 'old–new' dichotomy.
Constructing normative networks	Creating interorganisational connections so that new practices can be normatively sanctioned	Creation of expert groups, associations, and advocacy groups that evaluate and certify the innovation.
Mimicry	Associating new practices with existing sets of practices that are taken-for-granted.	Meshing the innovation with daily experiences. 'Just-a-better taxi'.
Theorising	With the development and specification of (new) abstract categories and the elaboration of causal chains	Creating scientific models and predictions, a new language to describe the practice. Such as the association with the 'sharing economy', 'ownership to access', etc.
Educating	Teaching actors new skills and knowledge related to supporting the new institutions.	Public outreach campaigns, information material, free test rides, etc.
Mythologising	Preserving the normative underpinning of an institution by creating and sustaining myths regarding its history	The stories about the 'great' men, high earnings, and efficiency gains.

Adapted from Binz et al. (2016) and Fuenfschilling and Truffer (2016).

the observed actions of (some of) the TNCs in the FHV industry. As we argue that TNCs represent a new component in FHV markets rather than something new, this framework shows that the components of the actions undertaken by the TNCs have much in common with institutional entrepreneurship, as argued by Pelzer et al. (2019). In this, the important factors are to change the regulations (or the regime) to fit the new service providers as opposed to providing a different service, although this is probably a question of degrees along a spectrum as opposed to a dichotomous distinction.

Regulatory Capture

Further to the concept of political economics, and related to the concept of authority prioritisation, is that of regulatory capture. The concept refers to a 'partisan' application of regulation that may differ from the interests of a wider community to focus on the interest of an individual or corporation. In the taxi industry, this can be framed as an accusation of unfairness, most commonly between the regulator and vehicle operator/company, the regulator being 'captured' or under the enthral of the supplier rather than the consumer.

Capture can occur where specific groups hold an increased stake in the outcome of a regulatory decision, giving that group an incentive to lobby for a particular outcome. The impact of capture can be harmful but may only be fully visible post the event. Thus, a public gain achieved in the short term, such as a reduction in fares, may actually result in long-term harm, where a supplier achieves a monopolistic position as a result of the initial discounting. To be fair, the regulator would need to balance both, even where public calls for short-term gains may be highly vocal.

The issue of regulatory capture becomes significant insofar as it relates to the extent of harm to the general public and may appear counter-intuitive at some points in its prosecution.

Notes

1 Some regulatory controls are applied to fares charged by TNCs, including the requirement to display fares in advance of travel as well as caps placed on surcharges, sometimes referred to as 'surge pricing' amongst TNCs.
2 While defined prices, set via a tariff or similar system, are usually able to remove monopolistic abuses at the point of use, the presence of a tariff does not remove the possible misstatement of fare that may occur, whether by accident or design. Some tariffs and taximeters are open to mistaken use through misallocation of tariff, where for example different daytime and nighttime fares exist, or where manual allocation of extras are required.
3 https://content.tfl.gov.uk/taxi-conditions-of-fitness-update-2019.pdf.

References

Agarwal, S., Diao, M., Pan, J. and Sing, T.F., (2015) *Are Singaporean cabdrivers target earners?* Available at SSRN: 2338476.

Arnott, R., (1996) 'Taxi travel should be subsidized', *Journal of Urban Economics*, 40(3), pp. 316–333. doi:10.1006/juec.1996.0035

Bekka, A., Louvet, N. and Adoue, F., (2020) 'Impact of a ridesourcing service on car ownership and resulting effects on vehicle kilometers travelled in the Paris Region', *Case Studies on Transport Policy*, 8, pp. 1010–1018. doi:10.1016/ j.cstp.2020.04.005

Bekken, J.-T. and Longva, F., (2003) *Impact of taxi market regulation—an international comparison*, TØI-report, 658/2003, Oslo: Institute of Transport Economics.

Binz, C., Harris-Lovett, S., Kiparsky, M., Sedlack, D.L. and Truffer, B., (2016) 'The thorny road to technology legitimation—Institutional work for potable water reuse in California', *Technological Forecasting and Social Change*, 103, pp. 249–263. doi:10.1016/j.techfore.2015.10.005

Camerer, C., Babcock, L., Loewenstein, G. and Thaler, R., (1997) 'Labor supply of New York City cabdrivers: One day at a time', *The Quarterly Journal of Economics*, 112, pp. 407–441. doi:10.1162/003355397555244

Cutolo, D. and Kenney, M., (2019) *Platform-dependent entrepreneurs: Power asymmetries, risks, and strategies in the platform economy.* Available at SSRN: https:// ssrn.com/ abstract=3372560. doi:10.2139/ssrn.3372560

Dempsey, P.S., (1996) 'Taxi industry regulation, deregulation, and reregulation: The paradox of market failure', *University of Denver College of Law, Transportation Law Journal*, 24(1), pp. 73–120. Available at SSRN: https://ssrn.com/abstract=2241306

Farber, H.S., (2015) 'Why you can't find a taxi in the rain and other labor supply lessons from cab drivers', *The Quarterly Journal of Economics*, 130, pp. 1975–2026.

Fuenfschilling, L. and Truffer, B., (2016) 'The interplay of institutions, actors and technologies in socio-technical systems—An analysis of transformations in the Australian urban water sector', *Technological Forecasting and Social Change*, 103, pp. 298–312. doi:10.1016/j.techfore.2015.11.023

Goldfarb, A. and Tucker, C., (2019) 'Digital economics', *Journal of Economic Literature*, 57, pp. 3–43.

Gwilliam, K., (2008) 'Bus transport: Is there a regulatory cycle?', *Transportation Research Part A: Policy and Practice*, 42(9), pp. 1183–1194. doi:10.1016/j.tra.2008.05.001

International Transport Forum, (2020) 'Good to go? Assessing the environmental performance of new mobility', *International Transport Forum Policy Papers*, No. 86. Paris: OECD Publishing. doi:10.1787/f5cd236b-en.

Kenney, M. and Zysman, J., (2016) 'The rise of the platform economy', *Issues in Science and Technology*, 32, p. 61.

Lawrence, T.B. and Suddaby, R., (2006) *The SAGE handbook of organization studies.* 2nd ed., pp. 215–254. London: SAGE Publications Ltd.

Mohring, H., (1972) 'Optimization and scale economies in urban bus transportation', *The American Economic Review*, 62(4), pp. 591–604.

Needham, D., (1983) *The economics and politics of regulation: A behavioural approach.* Boston, MA: Little, Brown.

Oppegaard, S.M.N., (2021) 'Regulating flexibility: Uber's platform as a technological work arrangement', *Nordic Journal of Working Life Studies*, 11, pp. 109–127.

Pelzer, P., Frenken, K. and Boon, W., (2019) 'Institutional entrepreneurship in the platform economy: How Uber tried (and failed) to change the Dutch taxi law', *Environmental Innovation and Societal Transitions*, 33, pp. 1–12. doi:10.1016/ j.eist.2019.02.003

Rayle, L., Dai, D., Chan, N., Cervero, R. and Shaheen, S., (2016) 'Just a better taxi? A survey-based comparison of taxis, transit, and ridesourcing services in San Francisco', *Transport Policy*, 45, pp. 168–178.

Rochet, J.-C. and Tirole, J., (2003) 'Platform competition in two-sided markets', *Journal of the European Economic Association*, 1, pp. 990–1029. doi:10.1162/1542476 03322493212

Schaller, B., (2017) 'Unsustainable? The growth of app-based ride services and traffic, travel and the future of New York City', *Report by Schaller Consulting*, Brooklyn, NY.

Shreiber, C., (1975) 'The economic reasons for price and entry regulation of taxi-cabs', *Journal of Transport Economics and Policy*, 9, pp. 268–279.

5   Industry Structure

The taxi industry has been dominated for much of its history by small companies with few employees. Most drivers are either self-employed (owner operator) or working in partnership with another (shared/lease driver). The large number of, nominally, independent suppliers appears, at least on the surface, to match textbook definitions of a competitive market. The structure has both historical and economic reasons for its form, alongside a regulated requirement, in some locations, to comply with defined ownership and control models. The most common structures observed in the traditional industry are being dominated by (taxi/vehicle) owners who also drive their vehicles.

While the multiplicity of many owner operators may create the theoretical conditions for competition, the historic structure has also resulted in a fragmented industry structure, without a single common voice or identity where it can be difficult to get an overview of the industry or the behavioural choices of its actors at a supply level.

Historical attempts to create single-unit entities, such as that of the early Hertz corporation (Cooper et al., 2016), have mostly failed. The conglomerate/larger companies tend to lose out in competition with smaller companies, owner operators, and vehicle leasers, mainly as a result of the limited economies of scale in vehicle operation. Pagano and McKnight (1983) observed that the efficient scale for taxi operation is reached at very modest scales (at the time of their observation).

Traditional economic arguments relate the underlying concentration on smaller enterprises and self-employment to the fact that it can be difficult to observe the amount of effort a driver puts in, with income frequently matched through the regulatory process to the effort put in by the driver, placing the vehicle at the right place at the right time and the direct cost of its provision. The reality is based on owner operators and/or vehicle lessors out-competing larger organisational forms.

In instances where an employer–employee relationship does exist, one of two models exists, where the driver receives a defined income from the owner, with all 'farebox' revenue going to the 'employer' or its counterpart

DOI: 10.4324/9781003256311-6

where all farebox revenue remains with the driver, who pays a defined fee for the vehicle (weigh-in). These structures are stable and have remained broadly unchanged over time in the traditional industry.

New market entrants, such as transportation network companies (TNCs), have the benefit of a more adaptable technology base. TNCs have more typically relied on better information exchanges to supplement driver 'wages' as a proportion of earnings by a complicated bonus and incentive structure, though the majority of TNCs continue to maintain a contractor relationship rather than being seen directly as employers. TNC bonuses can include extra payment for reaching a predefined number of trips, keeping the vehicle available for extra hours, moving the vehicle to an area with more demand, and so on: frequently allied to TNC service development, including the launch of new platform options and a maximisation of vehicle utilisation, consistent with its classification as a resource to the TNC, as opposed to the individual resource to the driver or owner operator in the case of the traditional taxi.

In contrast to the fragmented structure of individual vehicle operations in the taxi hail market, discussed below, vehicle dispatch services have strong economies of scale which will probably grow further with advances in the dispatch technologies on which they rely. As a result, competing pressures exist side by side across the industry both towards a highly fragmented structure in vehicle operation and a highly concentrated structure in vehicle coordination. In the subsequent section, this is described as a series of devolutions following technological developments in hailing.

Industry vs. Regulatory Structure

A correlation can be drawn between the structure of the industry, effectively its supply, and its regulated constraints, as one informs the other. In the following sections, we describe unique operational distinctions, primarily focused on the method of engagement – the method by which a passenger hires their vehicle. The same concept, of engagement method, is also common amongst defined categories, of vehicle, with some operating categories granted exclusive access to specific engagement methods.

The result has been the definition of licence 'tiers'. A single-tier system related to a single category of vehicle licence (i.e. all for hire vehicles [FHVs]), dual and multi-tiered systems permitting differential access to the market segments, dependent upon the tier to which a vehicle is associated. Dual-tier systems are common, typically taxi and private hire categorised separately, and thus able to serve different segments according to their category. The introduction of TNCs, as a separate tier, is more common in the USA and Canada than in Europe, creating three tiers in many US cities, while some EU counties may have further and additional categories for taxibus and other licensed vehicle types.

Street Hail

The street hail market is often seen as the most common within the taxi industry, though it need not necessarily represent the highest proportion by passenger number across all taxi markets. The street hail segment is distinct, based on the action of hailing a taxi, usually by summoning a vacant passing vehicle by a wave or hand movement. The vehicle is said to be plying-for-hire, *US Eng:* cruising, while the passenger hailing action can be called flagging. When hailing a vehicle for hire on the street, there is little need for advanced technology. A hand signal is usually enough, with some app companies pursuing electronic hailing (e-hail) as a method of approximating the process of street hail on an app platform.

Hailed vehicles will usually apply common fares, though various forms of 'tariff' can exist. Distinct exceptions to this can be seen, a good example being Gothenburg, Sweden, where fares are deregulated. Each Gothenburg taxi is required to prominently display a fare table including typical and maximum fares to allow a passenger to choose a taxi based on fare comparisons. The actual ability to make this choice may be limited in the street-hail market.

In the majority of locations, street-hail fares and tariffs are defined in advance, often as maxima, though this does not exclude negotiations between driver and passenger. The actual ability to negotiate is also limited particularly where the measurement of time and distance is based on the use of taximeters, the use of metre conveying legitimacy to the passenger of fare accuracy.

The street-hail market remains simple in concept and does not require any significant additional investment in dispatch technologies that induce costs that need to be shared between vehicles. There is little need to create complex industry structures for the hail market alone.

In some locations, the hailed market is restricted to vehicles classified as taxis only and would exclude private hire, limousine, or TNCs in these instances.

Vehicles are typically owned and operated by owner operators or small- or medium-sized companies, leasing the vehicles to the driver on short-term contracts. Taximeter standards are normally set by local licensing authorities to protect customers in a market with strong information asymmetries.

Pre-booking/Advanced Booking/Dispatch Segment

The dispatch segment, in which a booking is required and vehicle is dispatched centrally, is more complex than hailing. The segment is focused on the dispatching entity, which can be a company, corporation, or cooperative, that connects and coordinates supply and demand. In some locations, the segment is allied to a physical central office or base, including garages, but can also include fleets which serve both dispatch and hailed markets.

Figure 5.1 Street-hail market schematic.

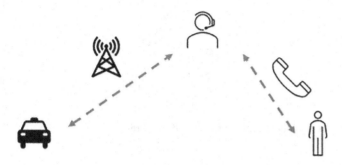

Figure 5.2 Schematic of a simple pre-book system c. 1950s to present.

The dispatch segment is illustrated in Figure 5.1 and will often be available to a wider range of vehicle licensing categories than the hailed market. Legal terms applied to the segment vary by location but can include private hire cars (PHVs), car services, and limousine services, discussed in more detail in the preceding chapters (Figure 5.2).

In the simplest form, the potential passenger calls the dispatcher who then coordinates supply. This has long been the main mode of operations for the minicab or limousine sectors. This market segment can work with phone, pen and paper, or more advanced technologies but require staff, and associated costs, or call takers and other non-driving personnel. This means that a proportion of the revenue from the trip needs to be set aside to cover the costs of the dispatch elements.

As larger dispatch services can achieve economies of scale, as described above, coordinating becomes increasingly complex that had resulted in a u-shaped cost curve, before the introduction of computers (Pagano and McKnight, 1983), increasing pressures to operate efficiently, typically through technology enhancements, with a large growth in supporting computer technologies seen in the 1990s.

Dispatcher Controlled

Adding computers to dispatching increases efficiency and allows for automatic processing of bookings. This can come in addition to the manually

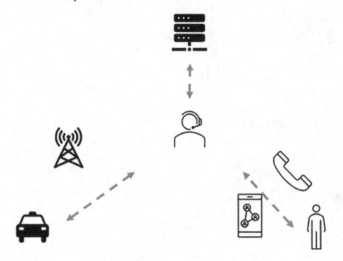

Figure 5.3 Schematic of computer-aided dispatch 1990 to present.

controlled bookings processed by a call centre, as illustrated in Figure 5.3. It also increases the trip-independent cost of operating a dispatching service.

As computing power increased and data transmission became possible through mobile phone networks, initially 2G/GSM networks, it became possible to transmit booking information directly to vehicle equipment. Vehicle displays have developed from simple display screens to more complex terminals, to integrated metre and data equipment, most recently focused on the phone itself.

The combination of data terminals and computer-supported dispatchers allowed the scale of operation and dispatcher efficiencies to be realised. It also created a new industry for software to support taxi bookings, including some originating from card payment backgrounds, allowing for the latter integration of payment systems, though these typically created their own costs and became subject to controversy related to external charges applied.

Software could be licensed to dispatch companies, changing the opportunity and scale of dispatch capability. Companies could now move from a city scale to that of a national or multi-national company, though such moves were usually accompanied by the retention of regional call centres, sometimes as a licence requirement. Standard bookings no longer required a local presence and have since developed to include cloud computing services.

App-based Dispatch

The arrival of 3G, 4G, and 5G data networks has brought with them significantly greater opportunities for large data flows across the dispatch system. More data can now be transmitted, at the same time, as the cost of, and need for, separate data terminals has fallen. Most dispatch features previously relying on dedicated data terminals can now operate on smartphones, with tablets also used where passenger-visible terminals are felt appropriate.

The advances in network and terminal technologies have also allowed a growth in cloud processing, the move from local physical to virtual servers, as illustrated in Figure 5.4. The system also permits a reduction in personnel, most commonly as a result of drivers and passengers communicating virtually without human intervention.

The move to a digital transaction, where interaction between the passenger and the driver becomes automated, has made it possible to bypass the traditional booking centre, creating a technological space where software technology companies can interact directly with both passengers and drivers. On the flip side, the automisation of the booking services has required more advanced programming capacity, and an increase fixed cost compared to earlier booking systems, but will result in minimal marginal costs, often close to zero, for processing each booking.

Automated and cloud systems have, in turn, catalysed the reorganisation of the supply side, particularly in the case of new market entrants, effectively transforming the industry. Platform-based dispatch becomes the norm for TNCs and many PHC companies but less so in the traditional taxi sector, particularly where the market has significant hailing, as these methods are less well suited to automated services.

In addition to the organisational changes created by better digital technologies, these have also created a series of other changes in the skills required in the industry, including:

- Better driver support through GPS location services, and live mapping apps, has reduced the need for the drivers to possess extensive knowledge of the local geography and street layouts;
- Better feedback systems, often referred to as ratings, have allowed passengers, drivers, and the TNC companies to exclude unwanted actors, without the need to involve regulators, though this has not been without controversy; and

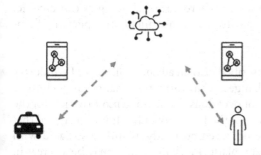

Figure 5.4 Schematic, cloud-based booking platforms (2010 to present).

- Online payment and defined fares in advance of travel have created a more certain payment environment, reducing no-shows of both passengers and drivers and a more secure structure for both the supplier and customer.

The transformation could also be described as the reallocation of services from a public good to a club good, where all involved parties and transactions are traceable. The potential/threat to be excluded from the service, for both drivers and passengers, has real consequences to behaviour, mainly positive, though some potential for malicious ratings can occur.

Impacts of Technology

The interaction between technological development and market outcome can be complex. It relies on the interplay between different actors, with different interests. It is not a linear process and may not be a result of the technology alone.

Multi-level Perspective (MLP) Analysis

A core observation in innovation studies is that technologies do not exist in a vacuum. They are surrounded by a technological regime that includes not only the specific technology and its protagonist but also a broader 'selection environment' which allows dominant technologies to stabilise and become accepted over time.

Geels (2002) suggests analysis of transformative change, and technological transitions, be approached using a theoretical framework, such as the MLP (Geels and Kemp, 2012). This framework can be used to understand the components of new technology implementation and its acceptance and take up in society. The MLP addresses three levels of analysis:

- Socio-technical landscape, which includes developments across sectors;
- The current socio-technical regime, including the technology itself, its area of science, policy, actors, institutions, culture, and industry associated with the use of a technology; and
- Niches, typically protected spaces where new technologies can emerge, sometimes referred to as incubators, but also including specialist fields and focused communities.

In previous chapters, we have described critical advances in the FHV industry associated with technological changes. Transformative changes in technologies have occurred on a number of occasions and include motorisation (of the vehicle) as well as the introduction of the two-way radio. It is also argued that a similar level of change can be observed currently, mainly associated with the development of online and app platforms. The change may be as great in impact or have a greater scope than motorisation.

As in the case of industrial transitions more generally, Geels and Schot (2007) argue that there are several conditions that need to be present at the same time for a transition to happen. If the conditions are not met, only minor changes are likely, there being no causal link between the development of a new technology and societal changes (changes in the socio-technical system). The FHV industry does, however, meet with conditions and can be observed against a number of mega-trends, changing the (socio-technical) landscape in which it operates. These include:

- Digitalisation, the steady progress of digital technologies;
- A shift in the focus from the purchase of goods to the consumption of services;
- Increased environmental awareness; and
- Urbanisation, amongst others.

Digitalisation has affected both the vehicles used and the interaction between drivers, passengers, and authorities and infrastructure. Digital technologies have improved existing vehicles, both by increasing comfort through driver assistance programs and reducing cost through increasing efficiency both in production and use of vehicles, though some of these efficiency gains may be offset by the use of larger and more complex vehicles.

The relationships between passengers and drivers have also changed, where technologies have lessened many of the information availability problems that have traditionally limited service provision efficiencies. These can relate to geography, where not knowing if there is a potential supply or demand nearby limits the number of trips made. This is solved by the transmission of both driver and passenger locations via the GPS location services integral to the platform or app. Quality and safety may also be enhanced, through the development of individual mutual rating systems, making it easier to identify a desirable driver and a paying passenger and exclude those felt undesirable or with a poor record of behaviour. Price and payment relationships are also enhanced by removing the price decision and payment transaction from the vehicle to the platform, often in the form of a pre-determined quoted fare, *aka: up-front fare.*

At the socio-technological regime level, there have also been several developments. The last decade has seen rapid change, following a long period with relatively little. Most are associated with acceptance and/or regulation of the emerging app market. Prior to widespread app use, circa 2012, vehicles would have drawn from a conventional auto-mobility system. Some adaptions could be seen to accommodate special needs, especially in terms of accessible vehicles, but little targeted science or technological development was common.

Policy has also remained stable over an extended period, with occasional forays into regulatory reform, following the concept of a regulatory cycle (Bekken and Longva, 2003; Gwilliam, 2008), discussed in the early chapters of this book. As a result, the industry had tended to remain stable with many of the same actors over extended periods. Companies and industrial structures could be said to have evolved slowly, while institutions that supported the industry, mainly regulatory bodies, remained local with little change. Effectively, the industry's culture had changed little over the period following the Great Depression in the 1930s.

Despite its apparent stability, several minor challenges can be seen. The perceived role, and legitimacy, of the regulators came under pressure, often from all sides. The political challenge was inked to net-liberalism, where public sector involvement in markets was becoming increasingly seen as problematic. Economic inefficiencies were also apparent and include high medallion prices (where taxi licences are capped and these are traded, showing a clear indication of rent-seeking behaviour from the suppliers) and an ongoing perception of low and varying service quality.

Taxi use, and its cultural significance, has also changed. Traditional taxis appear to be experiencing a decline against their competitors, while driver shortages and a loss of status may also be seen (Staalhane and Vassenden, 2022). The traditional industry has also been slow to adopt new technologies, with updates, as exist, focused on minor adjustments, vehicles with new fuels, and evolutionary changes to booking systems, which can compare poorly to TNCs, which have, in contrast, have created alternative socio-technical regimes by combining several of these innovations. TNCs, in particular, have successfully challenged the existing science, policy, actors, institutions, and culture surrounding the pre-existing vehicle for hire industry. A very important premise for this radical change has been the development and the adaption of the traditional IT sector organisational form, the digital platform. This form of organisation has been transferred from IT to a number of other sectors, including FHV.

Digital Platforms

Apart from the direct economic effects of digital technology, in particular the reduced cost of moving information, a major effect of digital technologies has been to allow different organisational structures.

Since 2010, much of the implication digitalisation has had on society has centred on the introduction of the digital platform as an organisational form. The platform being a relatively new phenomenon in historical context. Differences of opinion continue, as to how it should be defined, its status and identification, with many descriptions varying depending on context.

An important aspect of the digital platform is the creation of a virtual marketplace, between sellers and buyers, and offering a very different power structure compared to conventional markets. Although both, traditional and platform markets, can be seen as examples of two-sided markets (Rochet and Tirole, 2003), the platform sets the rules for interaction, rather than the externally regulated environment of its predecessors.

Similar platform developments can be seen across sectors (Kenney et al., 2019), with varying degrees of success. A key question being to what extent the digital platform, the TNC platform in the case of the FHV industry, represents something different from earlier organisational forms, as argued by many of its promoters, or is a special case of the corporation (Frenken and Fuenfschilling, 2020).

In the case of TNCs, the digital platforms represent a more scalable version of the dispatch company, often working internationally. The TNC maintains many of the characteristics of the pre-existing market, setting prices and defining quality in line with many private hire companies, while allowing drivers and passengers to decide quantity. A driver can, to some extent, choose whether to drive or which platform to log on to, and the passenger to take the trip or not or by which mode to travel. However, the short-term flexibility of both labour and demand may leave something to desire. Drivers may not have a long series of job opportunities waiting, and passengers may not have all that many mobility options.

Compared to other sectors where the digital platform has been introduced, the change in organisational structure is smaller in the FHV industry. Small-scale supply coordinated by intermediaries has a long history. In contrast to sectors as accommodation, where supply traditionally has been much more concentrated, the gig payment was also the norm from before the arrival of the platform-organised TNCs.

The direct technological effect of the digital platforms in the FHV industry has been that they have offered a similar or superior service within a familiar framework, both on the passenger and driver side.

However, digital platforms have challenged all elements of the pre-existing socio-technical regime to various degrees. Science has been challenged, both by providing a new phenomenon that is studied and by creating new science agendas. With technological development on behavioural analysis and autonomy being repositioned, a major shift has been related to the role of the public sector. Where public sector regulators have been replaced by on-platform regulations, there have also been numerous efforts in challenging existing regulations, creating new rules that better fit the interests of the TNCs (Pelzer et al., 2019). There have been efforts that have reduced the legitimacy of local regulations and regulators, replacing these with regulations at higher administrative levels, against the established practice and conventional wisdom of the pre-existing industry (Aarhaug, 2016). Digital platforms have also challenged the concept of a 'taxi' as a brand and directly the taxi industry as a service. In addition, established institutions within the traditional industry have been sidelined, including price-setting authorities and various other practical and administrative tasks relating to how the established industry worked.

Another important development has been to change the culture surrounding both use and supply of the service. TNCs have successfully reached users who would not enter a taxi. And similarly, they have managed to reduce the barrier towards becoming a driver. This has been done by playing into the sharing and part-time work conceptual framework, although the change may be more about perception than actual change (Meelen and Frenken, 2015; Frenken and Schor, 2017). In terms of industry, the major challenges have not been to the driver as a profession, although some will argue that it is being down-skilled. Private sector dispatchers have been challenged by a new technology for hailing, and a very low marginal cost alternative to their established technologies, pushing many of these out of business. Small-scale IT actors have been absorbed or out-competed. Medallion holders have lost the value of their assets. Traditional representatives have lost their influence and so on.

The effects of these developments are not all bad. In many cases, the changes include both obvious advantages and new potential pitfalls. When public sector regulators are replaced with a mix of algorithmic regulation and decentralised feedback systems, this allows the platforms better control over their drivers and passengers. In many cases, this increases both efficiency and perceived safety. At the same time, it is criticised for lack of transparency. The latter is particularly a problem for drivers who may be dependent on TNCs for their income.

An important aspect of the platform is that it scales well. TNCs require continuous updating and therefore a large set of skilled programmers, but most transactions can be automated, providing good return to scale.

Still, the passengers and drivers, with their demand and supply, have largely remained the same, although the share of FHV of the total mobility market has increased through a mix of replacing public transport and newly generated trips.

References

Aarhaug, J., (2016) *Taxis as a part of public transport, sustainable urban transport technical document #16*. Berlin: Deutsche Gesellschaft für Internationale Zusammenarbeit (GIZ). Available at: http://sutp.org/files/contents/documents/resources/B_Technical-Documents/GIZ_SUTP_TD16_Taxi_EN.pdf

Bekken, J.-T. and Longva, F., (2003) *Impact of taxi market regulation—an international comparison*, TØI-report, 658/2003. Oslo: Institute of Transport Economics.

Cooper, J., Mundy, R. and Nelson, J., (2016) *Taxi! Urban economies and the social and transport impacts of the taxicab*. London: Routledge.

Cutolo, D. and Kenney, M., (2019) *Platform-dependent entrepreneurs: Power asymmetries, risks, and strategies in the platform economy*. Available at SSRN: https:// ssrn.com/abstract=3372560. doi:10.2139/ssrn.3372560

Frenken, K. and Fuenfschilling, L. (2020) 'The rise of online platforms and the triumph of the corporation', *Sociologica*, 14(3), pp. 101–113.

Frenken, K. and Schor, J., (2017) 'Putting the sharing economy into perspective', *Environmental Innovation and Societal Transitions*, 23, pp. 3–10.

Geels, F., Kemp, R., Dudley, G. 2012. *The Multi-Level Perspective as a New Perspective for Studying Socio-Technical Transitions*, Frank Geels and René Kemp In: *Automobility in transition?: A socio-technical analysis of sustainable transport*, Studies in Sustainability transitions, Geels, F., Kemp, R., Dudley, G. & Lyons, G (Eds) London, Routledge, pp 49–79 ISBN 9780415885058 Published January 30, 2012

Geels, F.W., (2002) 'Technological transitions as evolutionary reconfiguration processes: A multi-level perspective and a case-study', *Research Policy*, 31, pp. 1257–1274. doi:10.1016/S0048-7333(02)00062-8

Geels, F.W. and Schot, J., (2007) 'Typology of sociotechnical transition pathways', *Research Policy*, 36, pp. 399–417. doi:10.1016/j.respol.2007.01.003

Gwilliam, K., (2008) 'Bus transport: Is there a regulatory cycle?', *Transportation Research Part A: Policy and Practice*, 42(9), pp. 1183–1194. doi:10.1016/j.tra.2008.05.001

Kenney, M., Rouvinen, P., Seppälä, T. and Zysman, J., (2019) 'Platforms and industrial change', *Industry and Innovation*, 26, pp. 871–879.

Meelan, T. and Frenken, K., (2015) 'Stop saying Uber is part of the sharing economy', *Fast Company*, 14 January 2015. Available at: https://www.fastcompany.com/3040863/stop-saying-uber-is-part-of-the-sharing-economy

Pagano, A.M. and McKnight, C.E., (1983) 'Economies of scale in the taxicab industry: Some empirical evidence from the United States', *Journal of Transport Economics and Policy*, 17(3), pp. 299–313.

Pelzer, P., Frenken, K. and Boon, W., (2019) 'Institutional entrepreneurship in the platform economy: How Uber tried (and failed) to change the Dutch taxi law', *Environmental Innovation and Societal Transitions*, 33, pp. 1–12. doi:10.1016/j.eist.2019.02.003

Rochet, J.-C. and Tirole, J., (2003) 'Platform competition in two-sided markets', *Journal of the European Economic Association*, 1, pp. 990–1029. doi:10.1162/154247603322493212

Staalhane, H.H. and Vassenden, A., (2022) 'A tailspin for taxi drivers: Platform labor, deregulations, and a migrant occupation', *Nordic Journal of Working Life Studies*, 12, doi:10.18291/njwls.129365

Wardman, M., Toner, J., Fearnley, N., Flügel, S. and Killi, M., (2018) 'Review and meta-analysis of inter-modal cross-elasticity evidence', *Transportation Research Part A: Policy and Practice*, 118, pp. 662–681. doi:10.1016/j.tra.2018.10.002

6 Societal Change, Public and Passenger Perspectives

Having established many of the frameworks within which the for hire vehicle (FHV) market operates, it is appropriate to review the perspectives, expectations, and aspirations of the travelling public and the wider societies within which services are provided.

Many of the regulatory constraints within which the FHV industry has developed allude to controls applied as being in the public interest. How therefore is this interest defined and measured? In posing this as a question, it is also possible to go further; as the models applied in some locations are assessment tools that support updates to the regulatory environment but have limited or even minimal, regard to changes in public behaviour. How then are the fundamentals of public choice accommodated, if indeed they are.

Observed cost models applied to the industry in a number of locations appear to be based on direct costs and may omit propensities to use – effectively numbers of trips and/or trip characteristics. Models supporting number restraint can include tools that consider population size and not trends in or changes to travel behaviour. Indeed, it is the absence of a more systematic and sympathetic assessment of public need that may have created the circumstances in which transport network companies (TNCs) could enter and excel. This was not the first time such a gap had been created by regulations, impacting on the FHV industry, nor is it likely to be the last.

In this section, we review the societal environments visible at each of the revolutionary points in the industry. These are listed using the terminologies established in preceding chapters, starting from the deregulatory movements of the 1970s to date. Earlier examples of social change, though prescient to each step change, are limited in this review to the historical example each provide. We present the differing approaches to FHV market control applied by country and region, using selected case studies to demonstrate where global outcomes have emerged, location-specific 'experiences' and their differences. Thus, the social change in the USA that followed the Great Depression brought mass entry to taxi supply, particularly in 1920s US markets, but in common with other locations also suffering from dramatic declines in traditional employment. The FHV industry appeared to offer relatively low barriers to entry, particularly in comparison with the acute shortages of employment

DOI: 10.4324/9781003256311-7

in administrative or manual employment. Cities were faced with significant deficits and were forced to reduce the public services they provided, including swingeing cuts to public transport, further increasing the number of unemployed drivers. This had the result that a flood of new drivers sought access to the, relatively uncontrolled, taxi industry. Cut-throat and destructive competition followed, as did the emergence of the jitney (shared taxi) as an affordable stand-in for public transport. The events did not always pass without conflict, leading to a call for effective regulations, with cities and authorities applying formal registration/licensing, quality, and quantity controls as a result.[1]

These changes can all be argued as creating significant impetus for and dramatic change in their own right. They are critical for an understanding of contact and baseline. Equally those occurring before them, including the dramatic shifts permitted by motorised transport as it replaced horses; or taximeters, which contributed to reliable pricing, amongst others, also provide backdrops for the current market. It is, however, the period since the 1970s that has set the scene for the current incarnation of change and thus may provide lessons and demonstrate future opportunities.

The Deregulatory Movement

By the late 1970s/early 1980s, both the USA and the UK had entered a period focused on deregulation, a neo-liberal concept favouring policies that promoted free-market capitalism. High levels of public ownership, at the time, were seen as less desirable and were followed by a period of privatisations and market liberalisations, primarily focused on nationalised industries and utilities, including transport. The strengthening of free-market capitalism reflected not only the ideologies of the administrations, under both Reagan and Thatcher governments on either side of the Atlantic, but also a period of declining productivities, inflationary pressures, and pressure to address falling corporate profitability.

Other European countries were set to follow in short order, but the significance of the change was particularly visible in its first incarnations. In 1978, the US opened its aviation market, under the US Airline Deregulation Act (Henig, 1989), with similar deregulation in Canada in 1984. The UK moved to liberalise and privatise its utility industries from the early 1980s. Highly visible examples include the sale of British Telecom, formerly part of the Post Office, in 1984; British Gas in 1986; and the deregulation of local bus services under the Transport Act 1985, creating a market for private bus operations and a prohibition of local authority ownership. Former municipal operations either moved to fully commercial provision outwith authority control; or, a limited number of, arm's length companies, private companies were owned by authorities but operated independently as commercial concerns.

The pressures to promote liberalisation, deregulation, and sale became stylised as a 'deregulatory movement' (Keeler, 1984) and is argued to reflect both economic and ideological motives.

Deregulation in the UK can also be allied to political pressures, tied to the manifesto commitments of the Thatcher governments (1979–1990), in much the same way as seen under the Reagan administration in the USA. Keeler (ibid.) also introduces the concept of special-interest lobbying. Craig (2016) focuses on the relative power of lobby groups both those for and against regulation, developing the view that interest groups, effectively lobby groups, would often work against the public interest, defining the concept and conflicts as Interest Group Theory. The extent to which the lobby groups were able to impact on policy direction reflected the relative powers of the interest groups in competition with each other. The same conflicts appear to remain an issue in the current round of regulatory reform.

Transport Deregulation

Public transport modes, including taxis, were not exempt from the deregulatory movement. The US Rail Passenger Service Act (1970) separated passenger services from track and freight operations, creating the National Railroad Passenger Corporation (NRPC), later renamed Amtrak, as a private entity that would receive taxpayer funding and assume operation of intercity passenger trains. Freight operators remained privately owned, freed of passenger service obligations under the 1970 act, and, crucially, retained ownership and primary use of the tracks. The UK Transport Act 1985 brought most of the country's bus network under private ownership, excluding Ulsterbus services.[2] Rail ownership in much of the UK moved towards private ownership from 1991, initially as a result of the EU directive 91/440, which also had effect in other EU countries, and in UK law under the Railways Act (1993), which applied to most but not all railway systems.[3] The 1993 act separated national track infrastructure from operations, moving tracks initially to Railtrack and latterly to Network Rail, while the trains themselves were allocated through a series of franchises granted to private operators who would bid for large groups of services, often geographically similar to the historical railway companies of Great Britain. Competing operators could seek direct competition through the allocation of open access 'paths' of which Grand Central and Hull Railways became used as examples (ORR, 2022), while a majority of competition was seen in separated and alternative routes from the same origins to the same destinations. Thus, Avanti rail would compete via its west coast route between London and Scotland with LNER who operate between London and Scotland using the East Coast Mainline.[4]

The taxi, though not strictly a 'nationalised' industry, had been subject to a series of 'burdensome' regulations from the early 1920s (Schaller, 2018) that brought the mode under a greater level of state control than would be likely in the open market. Taxi market interventions being designed to affect free-market outcomes of price and supply, the majority of the controls applied on the basis of public protection and many a result of the destructive competition seen in the industry in the 1920s USA.

For their part, the public had little say in the underlying regulatory structure, except insofar as it would be defined at a political and city administration level and thus generally subject to local government scrutiny. City administrations argued that the public could, and should, reasonably expect minimum service standards including for safety and avoidance of anticompetitive exploitation. The authority assumed the role as the 'neutral' arbiter of standards, and, in so doing, the role of determining standards, their measurement, and enforcement, with national legislation enforcement typically devolved to the municipal level.

Herein lies one of the potential conflicts. Not least that the same expectations, of public safety and protection, could reasonably be applied to most industries, a majority of which are not subject to a sector-specific regulator or municipal enforcement. Most issues of market abuse would reasonably be addressed through anticompetitive regulation (*US: Anti-trust*), and most basic car safety issues would be addressed through standardised vehicle inspections, neither relying on a localised industry-specific regulator. This raises the question as to how the FHV mode was different, say, to other forms of transport and why specific local regulation may be required for the taxi while the same was not required for other forms of passenger transport. Moreover, what effect public opinions may have had on the choice of regulatory structure, and overall willingness to accept specific market forms, despite their frequent and widespread application.

To understand the pressures at work, we can look at recent history, starting with the influences and pressures apparent at the time of taxi deregulations in the USA seen in the early 1980s. The 1980s demonstrated a recent attempt at deregulation, albeit it was abortive. Subsequent attempts include New Zealand (1989), Sweden (1990), the Netherlands (2000), and Finland (2017), discussed in more detail below.

Taxi Deregulation

Much is made of the apparent failure to deregulate the taxi industry in the 1980s (Schaller, 2018), or, more precisely, the failure of the various attempts to deregulate at the time. The reforms seen in the 1980s, including their reversal, continue to impact on the current market and may thus be usefully described as the first (modern) deregulatory wave, to be followed by further waves of reform, including those most recently associated with TNC entry. The nature of the reforms, including the extent to which deregulation was attempted/achieved is also pertinent to the discussion. To fully understand the changes in the taxi industry at the point of each wave, we also need to unpack a number of similar, but not identical concepts, allied to deregulation. The first is the concept of derestriction, specifically, in the taxi context, the removal, or softening, of regulations pertaining to quantity.

The period from 1916 to 1979 was typified by tight controls applied to taxi numbers in US cities. The controls were largely a result of, the desire to avoid, excess and destructive competition within the taxi market and between taxis and jitneys.[5] The controls applied strict limits to the numbers of vehicle licences and/or driver licences permitted to operate within the jurisdiction of the authority. The restraint, frequently referred to as a taxi cap, was, and continues to be, applied through the issuance of licences, often in the form of physical plate or medallion displayed on or within the vehicle and/or as a driver licence, badge, or certificate. The removal of these caps, their derestriction, is one of a number of options towards deregulation.

The second area of deregulation relates to a liberalisation of the market. In much the same way as derestriction, this removes or softens some areas of market intervention, in this case quality controls/constraints. Thus, constraints applied to vehicle age, condition, driver training, and even appearance can be softened as a form of liberalisation. It is important to note that this did not advocate the removal of all quality controls, particularly those applied to vehicle roadworthiness, and/or the need for a driver to pass a driving test, though the undertaking of such minimal required tests need not lie within a distinct 'taxi' authority.

A third area of deregulation relates to economic controls, applied to the definition of fare levels, as a market intervention. The regulated market will often see price limitations or tariffs determined by an authority, being the maximum fares a taxi operator may charge for their service. The deregulated market allows the operators to define their own prices, in competition with each other.

American Experience of Taxi Deregulation

US deregulations occurred in the period from 1979 to 1984 and can be defined as the first wave of (modern) deregulation. It saw a total of 22 US cities, including San Diego, Seattle, and Phoenix, amongst others, removing a majority of controls, effectively in all three areas of regulation, while maintaining minimal controls on vehicle standards. The form of deregulation chosen was perhaps more extreme than directly necessary, or possibly more directly impactful than would have been the case in a more graduated move from regulated to deregulated, though subtle differences do exist between locations, allowing some determination of nuances between cities. The San Diego deregulation being of interest in that it was accompanied by parallel growth of the jitney market (see Reinke, 1986), and a more restrained return to regulation, with attempts within the city to maintain price competition through a graduated form of price control on deregulation. San Diego is also one of the few US cities where a jitney market has been retained post reform. Cities in California have tended to maintain control of their own taxi regulations, though some have combined their regulatory agencies with those of neighbouring cities, San Diego being one such example, where the regulatory agency, the San Diego Metropolitan Transit System (SDMTS) also regulates taxis in its nine immediate neighbouring cities.[6] It is notable that the regulation of TNCs in California differs in that TNCs are regulated at a state-wide level by the California Public Utilities Commission (CAPUC), while most taxi regulation is undertaken by city and urban authorities, thus creating a conflict of scale and scope.

In San Diego, California, taxi regulation is devolved by the nine cities that comprise a majority of the San Diego Metropolitan Area to the regional transport authority, the MTS. The administration of taxis' functions devolved as a part of a wider regulatory reform of public transport services, occurring in 1990. The SDMTS took over as taxi regulatory authority from the police department. This had the effect that taxis would be regulated by the same entity as other public transport services. In addition to the city of San Diego, the MTS was given the authority to regulate eight neighbouring cities (San Diego MTS, 2020). This relieved the smaller cities the need and complexity of taxi regulations.

Around 2000, the taxi fleet were approximately 900 taxis in the city of San Diego, with a total of 1,100 across the wider area overseen by MTS. In addition to taxis, separate licences are issued for charter vehicles, sightseeing vehicles, NEMTs, and jitneys, also under the jurisdiction of the MTS. Each of these licence categories had its own set of requirements and medallions, and the vehicles are inspected by the MTS. Permit numbers have traditionally been defined under a needs assessment exercise but have since been derestricted and are transferable under administration of the MTS. This said, the licenses remain under the ownership of the constituent cities. Licences awarded within the geographical boundary of San Diego city are able to pick up outside San Diego, within the MTS area, but licences awarded in the other MTS cities are not allowed to pick up in San Diego.

The regulatory agency is fully funded from the licence fee and is limited to a cost recovery model, meaning that it is not permitted to make a profit.

The number of active taxi licences in the MTS area today is approximately half of its peak. There have, however, been major increases to the number of NEMT vehicles, felt to be linked to an emerging requirement for Medicaid-supported services to only use licensed vehicles.

San Diego MTS have no regulatory control over TNCs operating in their area. Cities in Arizona, in contrast to those in California, applied state-wide regulations to taxis as well as TNCs. In the first wave of deregulation, the state has been reported as comprehensive (Teal, 1986), with parallel deregulation across multiple transport modes all occurring in the same 'wave'. Teal (ibid.) notes:

> 'the entire motor vehicle common carriage industry in the state was deregulated in mid-1982. This includes trucks, buses, taxis, airport vehicles, and the like.'... The deregulation was complete'... with ... 'no entry restrictions, no exit restrictions, no pricing restrictions, no service standards.'

Seattle is also often quoted in reviews of taxi deregulation (Doxsey, 1986). The city is notable for several reasons, not least that the city had shared its regulatory functions with its immediate neighbour, King County. The onset of deregulation resulted in a break with the county, moving shared regulation and reciprocal agreement to individual regulation, by both the city and the county, though the reciprocal arrangements were returned as the city re-regulated its industry. The city is also appropriate to discussion in respect of its development of formula-based price regulation, a direct outcome and attempt to regularise price control after re-regulation, and the existence of an additional vehicle category, the private for hire market, bearing similarities to the limousine and black car segments in other cities but separate from these as an additional category in its own right.

Washington DC is a special case in the US. The administrative area is defined as a district rather than a city and comprises a large proportion of the urban area with which it is associated.[7] The district is geographically small at 177 km^2 and densely populated; it is closely connected with the neighbouring states.

Before 2010, there had been a prolonged period of turmoil in the FHV industry in the city, a significant and widely quoted example being the use of a zonal fare system, rather than a metered version. This system was uniform for all FHVs. These were all legally regulated as PHVs. PHV licences were valid for one year and had to be renewed manually by physical presence.

All vehicles had a compulsory membership with a payment service provider (PSP), who logged all trips and collected revenue. There were a handful of competing PSPs, funded by membership fees. Vehicle owners could choose which to join. The PSPs were in turn audited by the taxi commission, which was appointed from the mayor's office (the mayor in DC having functions similar to that of a governor in other states).

The complexity of the situation was further amplified by the arrival of TNCs. Together this created a situation with possibilities for some creative solutions. Although there were developments similar to those observed in other US cities, with crackdowns and extensive ticketing of TNC drivers, this was relatively less conflicting than in other cities. Many of the TNC vehicles were registered as PHVs and complied by regulations. There were issues with unlicensed and uninsured vehicles. There was also a drop in demand for the pre-existing services, estimated to approximately 10%. However, this was to some extent compensated with increased demand for NEMT transport. Some of the NEMT services were moved from public service provision to competitive tendering procurements. The tenders were won by taxi companies, which were subsequently acquired by the DoT.

Cervero (1985) notes that all 22 of the first wave deregulated cities returned to (some form of) regulated markets within 3–5 years, with many commentators drawing the, reasonably logical, conclusion that deregulation of the industry had not worked. The restoration of regulation being taken as vindication of its need in many reviews, while others developed theories concerning the social factors at play in the success, or otherwise, of the de-regulatory 'experiment'. Teal and Berglund (1987) observed that the change had led to an atomisation of the industry, a higher number of vehicles, adding to a loss of centralised control. The same authors noted that deregulation had not achieved the results used in its justification, resulting in higher fares, rather than price competition, despite the relative increase in supply. Passengers remained unlikely to shop around, continuing a traditional pattern of use, concluding it was...

> very doubtful whether taxi consumers possess[ed] the information on price and services offerings needed to establish an truly competitive market for the telephone order [pre-booked] portion of the taxi industry...

Information asymmetry continues to be an issue and relates to the relative inability of a consumer to compare prices ahead of travel. The fact that a consumer has limited access to price data continues to be one of the most persuasive justifications for price and fare controls applied in most licensing authority areas but should also be treated with scepticism both in terms of its absolute validity and in relation to claims that technologies have replaced the need for absolute controls. An allied argument may apply to the appearance of competitive pricing and the concept of 'fare-washing' being the presentation of best value, whether demonstrating best value relates to its reality or not. Similar arguments exist in the current market in terms of market price supplements said to support increased supply or market matching through active fare hikes.

Teal and Berglund (ibid.) also assessed the impacts of deregulation on consumer choice, suggesting that the most frequently cited reason for a passenger to choose a specific operator ..."*was familiarity with the provider. This factor was quoted five times as often as low price*". Effectively that the public were more likely to value their perception of an operator's quality than an informed decision on price. Indeed, to obtain information on price was likely to be an arduous process, where tariffs had become opaque, and continued to remain complex in their presentation. In reality, tariff-based fares did and continue to require knowledge of both trip time and distance, specific knowledge of extra charges and supplements that where charged in their calculation, to an extent unlikely in most uses. This makes their computation all but impossible at time of use. It is also noted that regardless of the complexity of the tariff, their fundamental accuracy also relies on the underlying honesty of the driver to take the shortest route.

For their part, drivers rarely saw benefit in price competition at point of use. From the perception of a waiting taxi driver, a lower fare was simply that, less income from each and every trip. Driver self-interest, different to industry self-interest, would seek to charge as much as they could for each individual trip, further adding to the importance of reliability or honesty of a company in the view of the passenger. The perception of company honesty and reliability would play a role in the successes of app company growth in more recent history.

While there may be parallels between the deregulations of the 1980s and those of more recent years, they are not equal nor directly comparable. To establish the relative impacts, we need to establish lessons from the earlier deregulations and the impact of public responses the period since.

European Experience of Taxi Deregulation

Deregulation in European cities and states followed from the late 1980s and early 1990s, dependent upon the locations and prevailing politics of the time, creating a second wave of deregulation.

Belgium

Taxi regulations in Belgium are split between three administrative regions: Flanders, Wallonia, and the Brussels region, who all control their taxi regulation independently. The region roughly matches the language-based governments of the country, though some distinctions are apparent, discussed in relation to the taxi industry below.

The Brussels region introduced a series of revised taxi regulations only recently, being effective from 21 October 2022, the new regulations appear to be inspired by and follow many of the principles of a similarly recent reform adopted in the Flanders Region, effective from 1 January 2020. Both the approach adopted by the Brussels region and that of Flanders maintain an element of regulatory quantity control but both ease entry limitation significantly.

The 2022 reforms applied to Brussels replace a regulatory framework applied in 1995. It recognises the entry of TNCs to the market from 2014. Significantly, the new regulations move away from the classification of TNCs as limousines (VVB licence) and ends pre-booked requirements, including a theoretical need for the vehicle to be (pre)booked for a minimum of 3 hours and carry proof of each 'job' in the vehicle.

It is also important to note the geographical context of the Brussels market, as an enclave surrounded by the much larger regions of Flanders and Wallonia. TNC drivers who had been unable to get a Brussels VVB licence would be able to apply to the neighbouring authority and still work in the Belgian capital.

TNC operations were strenuously opposed to TNC entry. An early TNC segment, UberPOP, was opposed, as was the use of 'limousines' and the VVB licence by platform drivers, with such uses claimed to be illegal. Numerous legal actions were taken against TNC operators, which at various times decided TNCs could not receive orders by mobile phone, the final such case concluding, at the Brussels Court of Appeal, that a TNC had been operating illegally in the Brussels between 2015 and 2021. The culmination of legal action being the suspension of TNC services, albeit for a relatively short period of time, and a reform of the differing branded segments available.

In its new taxi ordinance, the Brussels City Region has adopted a series of reforms similar to those adopted in Flanders. The market now comprises two tiers. It creates a unified taxi sector and a level playing field with a common basic statute for rank taxis that can operate on demand, while platform taxis, predominantly TNCs, must be pre-booked.

Classic rank taxis are limited to a total of 1,425 vehicles and platform taxis to 1,825, to an upper limit of 3,250 vehicles. Of the 1,425 rank taxis, 140 must be e-taxis and 50 hydrogen-powered taxis. One hundred and fifty taxis (increasing to 200 over time) must be accessible. TNCs must offer 50 accessible vehicles, 50 electric, and 25 hydrogen vehicles. There are also 85 permits for luxury vehicles, the limousines.

Denmark

Copenhagen is the capital city of Denmark with approximately 1.4 million inhabitants. The city is located with its inner suburbs on the Danish side of the Øresund. It covers an area of 180 km^2. The city was served by 2,296 taxis in 2010.

Until its reform in 2018, the Danish taxi system had been highly regulated under a single-tier system. All taxis had been registered under the same category. In 2010, taxi fares and licence numbers were regulated at local government level, either by single municipalities or a collection of municipalities, as the case was in the Copenhagen area. Licences were limited to local operation, either within, to, or from the home area of the licence holder. Taxi licences were personal and non-transferable.

TNCs, specifically Uber, entered the Copenhagen markets in November 2014. The first regulatory response being to report their activities as unsanctioned to the police by the government traffic agency. Despite the actions of the regulator, the TNC continued to operate, while awaiting the outcome of trials against the drivers. Various legal actions were taken against the TNC drivers and the TNC itself.

The period included a number of trials and appeals, the regulator complaints being upheld in the Danish appeal court. This was further taken to the EU court but did not proceed before the parallel test case of Barcelona, discussed in the Spain section below. The Danish lawsuit against the TNC was finally settled in July 2020 when the TNC accepted to pay a fine estimated at 20% of the TNC revenue from activities in Denmark.

In parallel to the actions against the TNC, the country developed a new taxi regulation, which came into force on 1 January 2018. The new law included several changes from the previous regulations. First, it moved the licensing authority to the state and removed the local areas of operation. Restrictions on the number of permits were gradually removed, over a three-year period. So that, as of 2022, all qualified applicants will be awarded the number of licences they would like. Newly issued licences are valid across Denmark. However, the regulation stipulating a maximum fare was retained. As was components of the technical regulation requiring a taximeter, seat sensors, and video monitoring.

Until the new taxi law was implemented in 2018, the number of taxis operating in Copenhagen had remained largely stagnant at least since 2007. Directly following the new taxi law, the number increased to 2,719 in 2019 and 2,994 in 2020. Following the pandemic, the number of registered taxi vehicles in Copenhagen has dropped somewhat to 2,717 as of 2022 (Danmarks Statistik, 2022). Also, as of autumn 2022, no TNC is operating in Denmark.

Netherlands

Taxi deregulation was introduced in the Netherlands in 2000. Deregulation was intended to increase access to the market, making the profession easier to enter and making the taxi more attractive.

The reform removed capacity restraints and liberalised fare setting. Fares were limited to be below a defined ceiling (maximum fare), allowing operators to define their own tariffs below this rate. In practice, most operators chose a fare at or close to the fare ceiling. Access to the profession was simplified for drivers and access to the market virtually opened for operators.

Regulators defined quality-based practices, including a 'Quality Marque', that would be required of operators tendering for publicly supported social transportation, a significant proportion of all trips of between 75% and 80% by income.

Issues of discipline and control have emerged since the reform and have been addressed through the 'Toegelaten Taxi Organisatie' (TTO), Eng: Permitted Taxi Organisation; a further form of (self-regulated) quality marque. TTOs are permitted the use of unique roof lights and are intended to reduce conflict between operators.

Norway

By the early 1990s, the Norwegian capital, Oslo, operated a single tier taxi system that had resulted from a series of minor revisions in the period since its original inception in 1926. At the heart of the Oslo regulation was a control on vehicle numbers to ensure "a fair" compromise between the interests of the city and the industry. In the mid-1990s, the number of vehicles permitted was capped at 1,250. The Oslo market was distinct and organised through owner operator sole proprietorships, each with a one licence and one vehicle per owner. Licences were non-transferable, awarded for life (defined to a maximum of 70 years). New licence issuance occurred when an existing licence expired or was surrendered, or where the city council identified a need for greater numbers through infrequent review. New award was defined by seniority, using a list system.

By 1998, pressure had grown suggesting the existing system to be inefficient. A reform followed, allowing new privately owned dispatchers to enter the market, with a new licence allocation of 200 additional licences. In 2000, price regulation was discontinued, with further new dispatchers allocated new licences over the following decade, with the total number of licences reaching approximately 2,200 in 2014.

The positive effects of the Oslo reforms were partial, with an observed fragmentation emerging, where the original dispatch companies retained market dominance, while the 'new' dispatchers appeared to focus on street markets, and, to a lesser extent, competing for tendered non-emergency medical transport trips and airport work. The period also saw fare increases on the new entrants who had focused on street work, while the dispatch market remained more or less stable when adjusted for inflation (see Figure 6.1).

Passenger utilisation amongst new operators (time with passenger in vehicle/time available) dropped when measured over the same time period. Decline was steep, with a new equilibrium reached at about 15% utilisation,

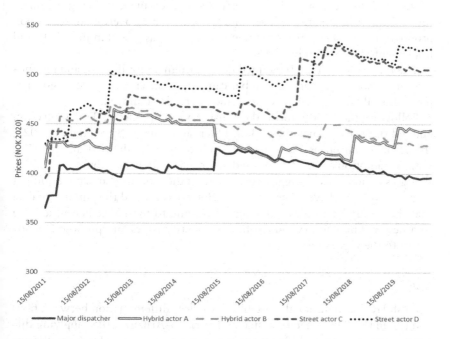

Figure 6.1 Fare rate comparison for a reference trip in Oslo (August 2011 to June 2020).
Source: Authors.

while remaining relatively high among the taxis operating with the main dispatcher, at around 40% (Aarhaug and Skollerud, 2019).

Much as seen in the US, a reversal of some aspects of the original reform was applied. In 2014, a new and stricter taxi regulation was adopted by the city council, aiming to reduce the number of vehicles to 1,500, at the same time as increasing the quality requirements for the vehicles and dispatchers.

The Oslo market was further changed by the arrival of its first major TNC, accompanied and supported by a strong publicity campaign targeting at existing taxi operators, politicians, and the public. The campaign presented a narrative of an old-fashioned and inefficient industry (including both operators and regulations), challenged by a modern and flexible new market entrant, followed by calls to discontinue licensing, control mechanisms, and other barriers to entry.

By 2017, a further disruption followed, with a Norwegian central government commitment to reform the legal framework under which cities and counties were able to regulate the FHV market, effectively a third wave change. The change followed a 2016 revelation by the Norwegian tax authorities that extensive tax evasion existed amongst TNC drivers, resulting in a pause to TNC market expansion and the launch of a public investigation on the sharing economy. The investigation recommended deregulation of the entire sector, at national level, and led to national government regulation proposals in October 2018. An amended version was passed in June 2019 and implemented in November 2020.

The taxi reform of 2020 retained the requirement for licences and taximeters but removed the vehicle number cap previously applied by local government. Locally defined quality guidelines were also removed.

Following the 2020 reform, the third wave, a number of TNCs have (re) entered the market, including: Bolt, Uber, and Yango. By September 2022, the number of licences operating in Oslo had increased dramatically to 4,716, with an additional 3,367 registered in the neighbouring county – Viken, though sporadic checks suggest that not all of these licences are active and not all active vehicles have a licence. The reform has limited the amount of data available, with the resulting market continuing to receive criticism, leading to a new public enquiry, established to identify issues and propose amendments to the regulation.

Spain

Spanish law has traditionally established a clear differentiation between taxis and the FHVs (Doménech-Pascual and Soriano-Arnanz, 2018) applying differing regulation to each. Regulation is applied at a regional level by the autonomous authorities (Comunidades Autónomos), with potential differences in legal regulation, definition, and application between the authorities.

The FHV market has traditionally been split into three operation/engagement modes, similar to those seen elsewhere:

- Hailed services that can ply-for-hire;
- A taxi rank segment; serving stands; and
- Dispatch services, hired by phone or electronic means.

And licensed in one of two categories:

- Taxis, available to all three engagement types; and
- Private hire, available to dispatch.

Related regulations apply by sector. Taxis are subject to driving time constraints and are required to take obligatory rest periods. This regulation does not apply to private hire. Equally taxi fares are controlled, while PHVs are not, and the taxi is generally subject to more stringent quality controls, though these differ by authority. The FHV market, both taxis and PHVs, is capped, with a maximum number of vehicles determined by the autonomous authority. In some instances an authority may apply a formula-based limitation to this regulation, illustrated in the case of Valencia, where, under article 7.4 of the Valencian Taxi Act, no new taxi authorisation may be granted in a municipality or joint area of taxi service provision when there is more than one taxi per 1,000 inhabitants.[8] Licences, thus issued, are transferable and may be bought and sold between operators.

Taxi vehicles have held the lion's share of the market, while PHVs have met demand for luxury and special services (ibid.). While the overall number of PHVs has significantly increased during the past few years, in January 2017, they still only represented 7.53% of the market.[9]

The market differs somewhat from other countries in that authorities are able, and do, to apply legal restrictions on the scale of taxi firms in addition to limits on the numbers of vehicles. Limits are applied in many authority areas on the number of licences a person may hold, the number of drivers a licensee can hire, and/or the number of vehicles a licensee can use.[10,11]

The Spanish experience of regulation is of particular interest both as an illustration of a, relatively, highly regulated market and in terms of legal challenges brought against new market entrants, specifically the case at the European Court Justice between a taxi company and a new entrant TNC. The case provided a reasoned judgement on the role of the TNC, as an intermediary (platform), and its status, whether the TNC could be defined as a transport company or a technology platform. The issue centred on company classification is discussed in the case of Association Professional Elite Taxi v. Uber Systems Spain SL in the Commercial Court 3 of Barcelona (2017) and its subsequent referral to the European Court of Justice (ECJ), in which the status of Uber as a transport company at all was adjudicated.

In the case of Elite Taxi vs. Uber Systems Spain SL, the ECJ judged that Uber (globally) acted as an 'intermediation service', providing a platform for the engagement of services, and this activity should be considered an integral part of the transport product. That despite the technological nature of the platform (EU Eng: ISS) and the differing domiciles of Uber BV and Rasier BV in the Netherlands. The outcome upheld the primacy of the Spanish authority in the regulation of the TNC as a local transport provider, rather than at an EU level, as a cross-boundary ISS company (de-Miguel-Molina et al., 2021)

Asian Experience of Taxi Deregulation

Singapore

The Singapore taxi market is regulated by the Land Transport Authority and currently defines its market into two tiers:

- Street hail – Taxis, permitted to ply for hire; and
- Ride hail – PHC, limousine, and P2P/TNC, permitted to accept dispatch via phone or app.

Street hail (taxis) must be fitted with a taximeter, complying to relevant standards, though fare rates are set by the individual taxi companies and are likely to differ between companies. Ride-hail trips are also open to price competition and may choose between metred or flat fares, as selected by the passenger.

The Singapore market experienced a limited operational deregulation under the Point-to-point Passenger Transport Industry Act 2019, and fare deregulation under the Public Transport Council (Street-hail Fare Pricing Policy) Order 2020. These included a standardisation of fare elements, though not the fare rate, and licence requirements for street-hail and ride-hail operations. Ride-hail requirements were defined for fleets over 800 vehicles. The Singapore Land Transport Authority confirmed five licensed ride-hail operators in 2022. Neither of the larger US TNCs operated in Singapore at the time of writing.

The market differs from its equivalents in the US, and many EU countries, insofar as taxis are able to accept both street-hail and TNC style of engagement by app, largely as a result of the placement of TNCs into the ride-hail category. This said, the taxi market is reported as having been in decline year on year for the last six years, while the ride-hail sector, including TNCs, has exceeded the street-hail market since 2016.

Australian Experience of Taxi Deregulation

Queensland

Before the arrival of TNCs in 2010, Queensland FHV regulation was split into several tiers, with taxis, private hire vehicles, and limousines as separate categories. The regulation had its origins in the Transport Operations Act of 1995. This was repeatedly amended. The regulation had strong support in both dominant political parties and the industry (Stein and Head, 2020).

The regulation included a maximum fare, restricted market access through tradable licences, and strong participation of the industry in the enforcement of the regulations. A centre piece in this regulation was a standardised matrix of minimum service levels (MSLs) and customer service requirements. These were monitored by the governments at dispatcher level. In other words, the dispatchers were both commercial actors and enforcers of regulation from the government. According to representatives of the industry and mystery shopper surveys, the industry was preforming very well. In 2010, the industry was mostly engaging with private customers through phone bookings. In 2014, the market was served by just over 60 dispatching companies, 23 of which were engaged in the contracts market, subject to the MSL.

Uber started operation in Brisbane, in early 2014, and went head-to-head with the existing industry and regulatory authorities. This created a series of conflicts. Uber drivers were fined. These fines were reportedly covered by Uber (Stein and Head, 2020). As Uber remained in the market, the value of the tradable taxi licences dropped. However, in this process, Uber gained traction politically and it became recognised within the political community, that the present regime with restricting entry was unsustainable (ibid.). This resulted in a review of the regulations. This process was parallel in other Australian states.

The resulting review and policy debate ended up with a new two-tier market system, with traditional taxis retaining the exclusive rights to street and stand hail, while the PHV segment became open entry.

Following this, the TNC gained market shares not only from previously unreached markets but also from previously established actors. However, over time, the difference in price and public perception between taxis and Uber and the later entrant Ola has decreased.

As of 2022, both tiers of service face similar issues with driver availability and quality (ibid.). There also seems to be a development towards an increasing split in the market where traditional taxis dominate on the street- and stand-hailing segments and on public contracts, while the TNCs, mainly Ola and Uber, dominate on the private pre-booking segments.

Stabilisation

In both the North American and European cases, early examples of deregulation did not always produce the results expected. The first wave deregulations in the US failed to achieve the market or competitive benefits initially promised, while the second wave, occurring in Europe, also appeared limited in achieving stated aims. In the event, the first wave of deregulation remained short lived. Deregulated cities returned to some form of control within five years; San Diego, which had deregulated in 1979, reimposed controls in 1984, with its counterparts in Seattle, Sacramento, Kansas City, Phoenix, and Oakland following a similar time trajectory (Cooper, 2016), though the precise nature of re-regulation differed slightly between locations.

Public responses appeared muted, with the first wave of deregulations failing to deliver significant price or quality benefits to consumers, with most cities reporting only limited growth in traffic, if any at all. The one area where deregulation had a significant impact had been the growth in the numbers of vehicles plying for hire, though this in itself created a difficulty – where numbers of passenger trips failed to grow, an increased pressure was placed on drivers to maximise income for every trip. The opportunity (incentive) for the (competitive) industry to win market share through lowering prices was lost to driver self-interest at the point of use, while quality competition was made unlikely by a declining per vehicle income – reducing quality enhancements rather than supporting them. The first wave of deregulation was followed by a cooling off period in which some level of stability was sought and regained through the re-emergence of regulatory control (Waterhouse, 1993).

Standardised approaches to regulation were developed, with model regulations proposed by some in the industry, and supported by the US taxi regulator association IATR. The market entered a period of stability, in the USA, and common approaches to fare measurement and supply controls in some. Concepts associated with convenience and necessity, requiring a measured justification of increased taxi licence numbers, were reported (Dempsey, 1996) in the USA, with a similar approach of measurement in the UK based on a standard assessment of Significant Unmet Demand (SUD) (DfT, 2010), while many cities sought a more ordered approach to fare setting. For its part, Seattle led the way towards a formula-based approach to fares in the USA (Leisy, 2019), adopting a multi-facet assessment of costs, using a taxi cost index to create a systematic review of fares based on industrial price indices (IPI) rather than operator-led applications for (opaque) fare increases (see: City of Chicago, 2014). Similar approaches to fare modelling, as well as a demand-oriented approach to supply, was visible in the UK at the same time, including a formalised approach to best practice issued by the UK DfT from 2006 (DfT, 2022).

Public and Market Effects

Public experience of taxi use would also stabilise, as the product became consistent or at least where destructive competition fell away. The period from 1985 to around 2010 was marked by evolutionary change, improved vehicle technologies, and discussions on the role of the mode in accessible transport. The link between the mode and accessibility being, and remaining, complicated by the relative costs of provision, demand, and duty to provide.

Other market effects, though evolutionary, include the move from analogue to digital communications, voice radio to data terminal, and the development of Internet bookings, as dispatch became a computerised and online activity.

Social transport would also be developed in the period, with increased links between the city(ies), their newly effective taxi regulators, and public commitments to social, school, health, and disability transport. This would typically be seen through the letting of transport provision contracts to taxi companies. European countries linked social transport agencies to the taxi fleet dispatch systems; Finland provided access to taxi transport through its social insurance agency: Kela, a case in point (Kauppila, 2015; Aapaoja et al., 2017), while dispatch operators could take advantage of reduced dispatch costs of new dispatch technologies.

The provision of accessible transport also moved forward in the period, though not evenly and certainly not without issue. In the US, the Americans with Disabilities Act (1990) (ADA) established a duty for transport authorities to provide parallel accessible transport; the parallel nature relating to the need to mirror bus and fixed route transit with an accessible service, giving rise to the US term 'Paratransit'. The ADA also requires FHV companies to make reasonable accommodation and support use, though the actual definition of 'reasonable' remained and continues to be ambiguous. The same concept, and similar legislation, appeared in other countries, with some cities providing all accessible fleets, including those where such requirements appear by historical coincidence as a part of previous regulation, the Metropolitan Conditions of Fitness is one such example.

The relative stability of the market allowed regulation to become commonplace and entrenched. Where visible, regulatory pressures sought to capitalise on the emergence of operational data, while competition within the market appeared to focus on market values, including the cost of medallions and their relative scarcity. Changes in the population, predominantly an increase in urban populations and associated demand for transport, were followed by reviews of taxi numbers and focused assessment of the role of the mode at key times, including in the Night Time Economy (NTE) (Smeds et al., 2020).

Onset Decline

The relative renaissance seen in the market from the onset of stabilisation was ultimately disturbed by the second and third deregulatory waves. To understand these fully, we have to review the potential and circumstances required for their success. The first being a gradual decline in the perceptions associated with the taxi mode.

For the travelling public, perceptions would become critical, with the realisation that the newly effective regulators would not always apply regulation evenly. Equally it can be argued that different customer groups, often differentiated by type, would not all benefit equally from service delivery. Perceptions were often allied to experience, with a lack of supply becoming an issue in some neighbourhoods. It needs to be underlined that any such absence would not necessarily reflect a decline in service but often an increasing expectation. In short, the supply side may not have become worse but rather the demand side sought more and/or better. By the 1990s, on both sides of the Atlantic, complaints were frequently made in respect of longer waiting times and an unwillingness to respond to shorter journey requests, described as journey refusals in the USA. Many of the same dynamics seen prior to re-regulation re-emerged, not least the conflict between the interests of the driver (as an individual) and the industry (as a collective). Drivers seeing low value short trips as a negative, typically not the ideal trip having waited at a stand or in a queue, while the public image of the industry became dominated by reported shortages in supply, poor service, and risk – particularly at taxi stands at night, despite a measured fall in violent crime of 19% (Rodden, 2017).

For their part, the operating companies may also have had an issue with the enforcement of regulations on numbers. Competing pressures emerged for the medallion market conflicts between the measurable increases in medallion price being a positive to the investor and a limitation to supply and earnings, particularly as the cost of medallions within the industry were set to hit their peak levels in the period 2010–2013, the highest of which, in New York City, exceeded a staggering $1million per licence. The New York market, amongst others, also demonstrated a potentially harmful link between the city, which gained significant income from the sale of medallions, and the maintenance of high traceable values, while the accusation of unhealthy links between the regulator and the industry also emerged, collectively 'regulatory capture' (Barrett, 2003). The same concept, of regulatory capture, would add to the pressure to deregulate and/or allow entry of TNCs in the third wave of deregulation (Adler, 2021), discussed below. The capital cost, of the medallion, would spawn crippling debt, through its associated medallion loans sector, and significant upward pressure on costs and, ultimately, driver livelihoods (Çetin and Eryigit, 2013).

The multiple sources of dissatisfaction to the public and operator appeared to have coalesced in the period from 2010 to 2013. Much of the frustration aimed at the regulatory structures, which by this stage had moved from the recovery of market balance necessary from the 1980s to a more contrived retention of unnecessary control. Benign regulator influences intended to protect the public interest could, by contrast, now appear to work against these goals: a view often reinforced by the regulators actions themselves, not least by the extended periods without increases in the numbers of licences issued, despite demographic changes that may have justified them and a similar cap on fares despite changes in operating costs. The emergence of market challengers in the third wave of deregulation, including Uber from 2010 and Lyft in 2012, would push at an open door, as a prelude to the many subsequent challenges the mode would face.

Challenger Entry

In the preceding sections, we have identified deregulation to have occurred in waves. The modern waves starting with the examples of deregulation in the USA in the 1980s ultimately failed to deliver on their promises and were reversed in relatively quick succession. The nature of the 'reversal' is important as it did not result in all authorities returning to exactly the same set of regulations that had been abandoned in their respective deregulations. The example of San Diego is important here as the city sought to retain price competition as an outcome of the regulatory change. This difference is important as it begins to suggest that the nature of deregulation had a role in its success (failure). The extreme nature of the first wave, choosing to deregulate across multiple areas of control, may have also had an impact on its ultimate reversal.

A second wave of deregulation followed at around the turn of the century, this time with a focus on European countries, often as a result of limited-service enhancement in the industry of the time. Norwegian deregulation occurred in 1998, see above, and was quickly followed by the Republic of Ireland, which deregulated all of its services in 2000.

The second wave is important as it predates the development of either the app or the TNC, highlighting a general dissatisfaction with the status quo, rather than emergence of the TNC, a market disrupter, as the primary driver of change. Dissatisfaction arising in many of the same areas had led to the first round of deregulation, undersupply, in specific circumstances, and a lack of visible improvement. Regulatory responses appeared muted with many of the tools adopted by the regulator in the interim appearing to lack the muscle to effect meaningful change.

Market Disruption

The third wave of deregulation, and possibly the most significant in industry since the 1920s, is directly associated with technological change. The emergence of the app-based service, and more specifically the emergence of the TNC company, created a significant change in both ability and structure of the industry.

While frequently conflated, the app technology and the TNC company are separate elements that both needed to be in place to create the circumstances for the third wave of deregulation. In the first instance, the app provides a facilitating technology that could, but need not necessarily, ferment change. The app itself being a result of the smartphone revolution, widely documented (Mallinson, 2015), and the catalyst of change across many differing industry sectors. In terms of its potential within the FHV market, the smartphone permits both a significantly enhanced processing opportunity at point of use and highly accurate location services. The combination of which, alongside effective cloud-based distribution and /or dispatch systems, can be seen to have redrawn what was possible in the delivery of transport services.

For their part, the taxi companies were slow to take up on the opportunities offered by the smartphone. The gap from its availability (from around

2007) to its wide-scale uptake, as TNCs, is indicative of the relatively limited interest of the traditional industry to explore the new technology. Those companies choosing to make use of a 'taxi app' before the wide-scale launch of TNCs were likely to have seen the technology as an add on, with multiple simplistic apps available, a majority of which failed to take advantage of the app technologies that could have been available to them. Kincaid (2008) observed:

> Taxi applications on the App Store are a dime a dozen, but for the most part they're just glorified phone directories that don't really make it any easier to call a cab.

Taxi companies appeared to lag behind other areas of transport, responding late, responding slowly, and responding weakly to the potential that apps could have had for their business, perhaps reflecting the relatively low importance of the app sector to the established business models in play at the time.

For their part, the TNC sector started its life as an alternative to existing limousine booking choices. The early platforms did not compete head on with the taxi trade but rather could be seen to support the dispatch of Black Car services. The relatively targeted market entry was quickly eclipsed by the demonstrated potential of the technology. Early entrant UberCab, challenged over its use of the word 'cab' in its title,[12] quickly moved to the more aggressive Uber Technologies and appeared to play off against its close US competitor Lyft to establish which would be able to master or excel in the vehicle dispatch app market. The competition between the two companies was critical to the market acceleration seen, as Lyft brought in the concept of non-professional drivers so too did its direct competitor. New market opportunities developed as TNC rivals moved to outdo each other in their search for new markets. The competition also ventured away from the relative certainty of the pre-existing market regulation to push into areas of regulatory ambiguity, a fact highlighted by the larger company in its white paper on the subject. The argument suggested that until regulatory certainty existed, the company would feel able, even obliged, to respond to its competition in the area of ambiguity. The period from 2012, and in particular launches in key cities such as San Francisco in 2012 and Seattle in 2013, tightened the competitive nature of the TNC market, giving the sector the image of an aggressive competitor across the wider FHV industry, both in reputation and reality.

Responses to Apps

Public response to TNC challengers has, despite numerous protestations, been one of welcome and enthusiasm. The TNC sector responded to the apparent inefficiencies of the incumbent operators, while undertaking a significant lobbying campaign in their own right.

For their part, the TNC challengers have been successful in creating a strong culture of 'them and us', with a majority of users being very much in favour of the new entrant, responding positively to the advances that the new apps brought. In the 'against' camp was the traditional industry and its regulators. The traditional sector was painted as staid and slow to respond, with some TNC advocates painting the traditional industry as 'big-taxi', a corporate behemoth using its corporate lobby power to limit public choice, while the reverse may actually have been the case. Regulators were painted with much the same brush, giving rise to accusations of regulatory capture, the complicity of the regulator in the interest of the traditional industry. The situation was made worse for the taxi industry, and its regulators, by their appearance of being prone, even adept, at falling in to bear traps set for them. Here too, as authors, it is hard not to state a side, as to avoid a viewpoint is *de facto* to express its opposite. Here then, we seek to describe the process of challenger entry, rather than pass judgement on its validity.

The creation of taxi-specific apps (taxi apps), rather than TNC, was given the label of 'legal apps' by the traditional industry. The taxi apps were frequently operated by a third party and would often fail to provide more than an online directory service. The nature of the relationship between the taxi company and app became caught up in controversy around the ownership of the client base, whether this lay with the app or the taxi company and a relative unwillingness of (some) operators to take the apps seriously. The first 'dispatching' app, Taxi Magic, launched in 2008 offering a mix of directory and direct booking services, though its critics would quickly point to a lack of supply, the use of distant, rather than nearest vehicles, and a complex payment structure that would often result in the passenger paying both the driver and app separately.[13]

The lack of traction for Taxi Magic would also reflect a lack of interest on the part of the industry. The traditional taxi company saw app bookings as only a minor part of their business, and potentially as an expensive side show, where additional fees would be paid to the app company rather than the taxi operator. The avoidance, by Uber, of direct competition with the taxi sector would also reinforce the separation, with the result that taxi apps became the poor relation of the app market, while the emerging TNCs could concentrate and excel.

App Market Failings

While convenient to look at the relative successes of the app market, in particular the significant improvement to customer services, the market is far from without controversy. Three areas of controversy are visible: the failure of the traditional market; the employment impacts of the changing environment, also presented as the emergence of the gig economy, whether good or bad; and the competitive impacts of the new market structure.

Taxi App Failings

In the preceding sections, we observed that the traditional market had been late to deliver app-based services. A primary factor, we suggested, being the relatively small proportion of the taxi market, at the time, using apps as an engagement tool. The lack of use remains visible, though the most recent generations of taxi app have gone some way to alleviate this. But it was the lead in from a head start to the current minor role that is worthy of unpacking.

The first point to consider is the geographical scale of the taxi industry. While the TNC has not been shy to illustrate their national and global ambitions, taxi companies appear much more likely to focus on the immediate cities in which they operate. Thus, a San Diego-based company is frequently just that. The observation is equally true in Glasgow – Glasgow Taxis; Edinburgh – Central Taxis and Citycabs; or London, as elsewhere. While groupings of taxi companies can exist, including the various YellowCab, operations in the USA only limited and somewhat belated efforts have been made to join booking services and create common apps. A lack of any significant national or global app presence has the effect that any visitor to a location is likely to need another app for that city, leading to crowded screens and an increasing lethargy to download yet again. Which app works where being more easily dealt with by the single TNC app that works (nearly) everywhere. The choice of app also relates to the concept of first screen choices, discussed elsewhere in this text, while many apps may simply not work given geo-blocking, the idea that only consumers from one geography should be able to use a spatially specific app, or simply a lack of knowledge on the part of the developer, and/ or an inability to recognise wider markets.

To be effective, the taxi app needed to be, and still needs, better than equivalence to have a chance to take significant market share. For the main part, taxi apps have not achieved this, with few prospects that they might.

Employment Rights and the Gig Economy

For their part, the TNC apps faced their own set of issues. The increase in market size, associated with the apps and taxi operating in parallel, increased demand for drivers and a subsequent increase in the use of workers in the 'gig economy'. To be accurate, it needs to be highlighted that the gig economy was not a result of app development but rather a historic term for a temporary employment, with early references from as far back as 1908, frequently used for theatrical and musical performances (Green, 1908). The term being well suited for the app sector where much employment is temporary, without set pattern and often required in response to specific requests.

It is also appropriate to highlight that, by the same definition, most traditional taxi drivers could also fall under the term of gig workers, though the term was rarely used for taxi drivers in the period prior to apps and only infrequently since. Both taxi and TNC drivers may be compared as private independent contractors, choosing to work as and when they wish, and only loosely associated with the company, scheme, or cooperative under whose name they may operate; though the nature of control applied by the TNC has led to a number of successful legal challenges to driver status, including in the UK Supreme Court: Uber BV and others (Appellants) v Aslam: Judgement (2021). In other locations, including California, the controversy has led to state-wide ballots to determine driver's rights, of which the California proposition 22 is an example. The California ballot being accompanied by very significant lobbying efforts, with TNC and app proponents contributing over $200 million to campaigns supporting the proposition, making it the most expensive ballot measure in California history to date.

At the heart of the gig economy argument are the employment rights afforded to TNC drivers. Permanent, and most temporary workers working on a contract, are guaranteed minimum working rights in law. These differ by location but will typically include entitlements to holidays, sick pay, and minimum wages in most locations. Gig economy workers are generally excluded from these rights, with only limited ability to request working standards outwith the driver's own control and severely limited rights to claim unfair dismissal. As a result, the early incarnations of drivers supplying the TNC app would be frequently provided on a part-time basis, often as an additional activity, or second job. The extent to which this remains the case is more questionable, the University of California Labor Center suggesting (UCLA, 2018) that around 2/3rds of TNC drivers rely on the TNC 'gig' as their primary source of income, with as many as half of the Los Angeles driver respondents suggesting that driving for TNCs was their only job.

Competitive Market Places

The final area where significant impacts may be identified relate to the competitive market place itself. The large-scale entry of TNCs has increased both public expectation of and reliance on apps as a form of engagement. The dominance of a limited number of app companies can, however, be problematic, particularly where price competition becomes limited. This does not, in and of itself, necessarily lead to a monopolistic situation, though it might, but rather forms a barrier to some users unable to use the app. In this way, the app fails to serve the unbanked, being the community unable, or unwilling, to hold a credit card or debit card (King et al., 2017); or those with specific accessibility needs sometimes not served by the more common app providers.

Other, tangential, market segments may also be impacted, particularly where an element of cross-subsidy existed between profitable and unprofitable service types, common amongst suburban supply, or where city Paratransit services might once have been contracted to suppliers who would now chose to concentrate on more profitable services (Koffman, 2016). Effectively the emergence of the TNC market could reduce opportunities in lower profit markets, though the opposite argument can, and has been made, in relation to market segments previously served poorly by the traditional taxi market (Mason and Menard, 2021) and a complex set of arguments around accessibility (Gonzales et al., 2019).

Notes

1 Quality control was not new at this point, nor indeed were quantity controls. The depression led to the reinforcement of existing concepts, and, in most cases, new, more stringent, quantity caps were applied in an effort to rein in extremes of competition.

2 UlsterBus, including CityBus in the Belfast metropolitan area, would be later re-branded as services of 'Translink', the 'national' transport operator for Northern Ireland, itself a nationalised umbrella company. Sub-branding of Translink also included Metro and Glider services amongst others.

3 Notable exceptions to the 1993 Railways Act privatisations include Northern Ireland Railways, to be later grouped under the 'Translink' banner, while remaining under public ownership and control as part of the government-operated Northern Ireland Transport Holding Company. Some mainland UK regional and local railways also remained separate from the 1993 act, including the Tyne and Wear Metro and London Underground, while later reclassifications and re-nationalisations include the London Overground, which moved under the control of Transport for London; Transport for Wales railway services; and the entirety of the Scotrail Network, which re-entered nationalised ownership in 2022.

4 The London to Edinburgh route is also served by the open access operator Lumo in direct competition to LNER serving many of the same stations. The corridor is also in direct competition with multiple airlines, with similar city centre to city centre travel times.

5 The concept of destructive competition is discussed in preceding chapters, while narratives of the jitney and taxi wars in individual cities is often chronicled by city; see also: Anderson (2016) for a review of the San Francisco market.

6 US city structures are often formed as metropolitan areas or groups of urban authorities around a central city. The regulator serves the wider conurbation.

7 For the avoidance of confusion, the majority of the 'Washington DC' city area falls within the District of Columbia. A small number of its immediate suburbs extend into its neighbouring states, primarily Maryland to the North of the River Potomac, and Virginia to the South. The extended metropolitan area is also contained within the three administrations: DC, Maryland and Virginia.

8 The precise definition of number, and its calculation differs between autonomous authorities. A further example being Article 6.2 of the Murcian Taxi Act 10/2014 of 27 November 2014 (Murcian Taxi Act), which establishes that municipalities are required to set out limits on the number of licenses.

9 According to the Observatory of Road Passenger Transport Services report 'Supply and Demand' in January 2017, there were 67,255 taxis and 5,473 PHV.

10 E.g.: art 8.2 Catalan Taxi Act 19/2003 limits a single person to the lower of 50 licenses; or a max of 15% of the total issued.

11 Some jurisdictions apply geographical restrictions on operating area, within the jurisdiction, sometimes called zones, see: West Dunbartonshire, Scotland; while others may place district-based service requirements, including 'Colors' schemes in San Francisco, amongst others.

12 Early challenges include the concept of passing off, as taxis, for example through the use of 'Cab' in a company title, whilst a common complaint suggested that

the easy (easier) dispatch of Limousine registered vehicles made them synony-
mous with taxis in the eyes of the public.
13 https://yourstory.com/2017/01/george-arison-taxi-magic/amp.

References

Aapaoja, A., Eckhardt, J., and Nykänen, L., (2017) 'Business models for MaaS', In
1st International Conference on Mobility as a Service. 28–29 November 2017. Tampere.
Tampere University of Technology.
Aarhaug, J., and Skollerud, K. H. (2019) *Taxi regulations in Norway – challenges and
alternative solutions,* TØI-report 1698/2019. Oslo, Institute of Transport Economics. Available at: https://www.toi.no/publikasjoner/drosjeregulering-i-nor-
ske-byer-utfordringer-og-alternativer-article35530-8.html
Adler, L., (2021) 'Framing disruption: How a regulatory capture frame legitimized
the deregulation of Boston's ride-for-hire industry', *Socio-Economic Review,* 19(4),
pp. 1421–1450. doi:10.1093/ ser/mwab020
Anderson, D., (2016) 'San Francisco's last Jitney has been driven out of business',
The third carriage age. Available at: http:// www.thirdcarriageage.com/2016/03/
san-franciscos-early-jitneys.html
Barrett, S.D., (2003), 'Regulatory capture, property rights and taxi deregulation: A
case study', *Economic Affairs,* 23, pp. 34–40. doi:10.1111/j.1468-0270.2003.00441.x
Cervero, R., (1985). Deregulating urban transportation. *Cato Journal,* 5, p. 219.
https://heinonline.org/HOL/LandingPage?handle=hein.journals/catoj5&div=
15&id=&page=
Çetin, T., and Eryigit, K.Y., (2013) 'The economic effects of government regulation:
Evidence from the New York taxicab market', *In Transport Policy,* 25, pp. 169–177.
ISSN 0967-070X, doi:10.1016/j.tranpol.2012.11.011
City of Chicago, (2014) *Taxi Fare Rate Study,* Available at: https://www.chicago.gov/
content/dam/city/depts/mayor/Press%20Room/
Cooper, J., Mundy, R. and Nelson, J., (2016) *Taxi! Urban economies and the social and
transport impacts of the taxicab.* London: Routledge.
Craig, J.D., (2016) 'Motivations for market restructuring: Evidence from U.S.
electricity deregulation', *Energy Economics,* 60, pp. 162–167. doi:10.1016/j.
eneco.2016.10.001
de-Miguel-Molina, M., de-Miguel-Molina, B. and Catalá-Pérez, D., (2021) 'The
collaborative economy and taxi services: Moving towards new business models in
Spain', *Research in Transportation Business and Management,* 39, 100503, ISSN 2210-
5395, doi:10.1016/j.rtbm.2020.100503
Dempsey, P.S., (1996) 'Taxi industry regulation, deregulation, and reregulation: The
paradox of market failure University of Denver College of Law', *Transportation Law
Journal,* 24(1), pp. 73–120. Available at SSRN: https://ssrn.com/abstract=2241306
DfT, (2010) UK Department for Transport. Best practice guidance for taxi and private hire licensing. Available at: https://assets.publishing.service.gov.uk/govern-
ment/ uploads/system/uploads/attachment_data/file/212554/taxi-pr
DfT, (2022) United Kingdom Department for Transport Taxi and Private Hire Vehicle Licensing: Best practice guidance for licensing authorities in England. Available
at: https://assets.publishing.service.gov.uk/government/ uploads/system/uploads/
attachment_data/file/1063053/taxi-and-private-hirevehicle-licensing-consult-
ing-on-best-practice-guidance-for-licensingauthorities-in-England.pdf

108   *Societal Change, Public and Passenger Perspectives*

Doménech Pascual, G. and Soriano Arnanz, A., (2018) 'Taxi regulation in spain under the pressure of the sharing econom', *Uber and Taxis Comparative Law Studies*, Bruylant, p. 357.

Doxsey, L., (1986) 'Interpreting the results of regulatory revisions in Seattle and San Diego', *Transportation Research Record*, 1103, pp. 6–8.

Gonzales, E.J., Sipetas, C. and Italiano, J.A., (2019) *Optimizing ADA Paratransit operation with taxis and ride share programs*. Report 19-004 MassDOT Massachusetts Department of transportation, May 2019. Available at: https://www.mass.gov/doc/optimizing-ada-paratransit-operations-with-taxi-and-ride-share-programs-0/download.

Green, H., (1908) *The Maison de Shine: More stories of the actors' boarding house*. New York: B. W. Dodge and Company.

Henig, J.R., (1989) 'Privatization in the United States: Theory and practice', *Political Science Quarterly*, 104(4), pp. 649–670. doi:10.2307/2151103

Kauppila, J., (2015) 'Publicly funded passenger transport services in Finland', *International Transport Forum Discussion Papers*, 2015(10). Paris: OECD Publishing. doi:10.1787/5jrvzrqmhc7h-en

Keeler, T.E., (1984) 'Theories of regulation and the deregulation movement', *Public Choice*, 44, pp. 103–145. doi:10.1007/BF00124820

Kincaid, J., (2008) 'Taxi magic: Hail a cab from your iPhone at the push of a button', *TechCrunch*, [Online] Available at: https://techcrunch.com/2008/12/16/taxi-magic-hail-a-cab-from-your-iphone-at-the-push-of-a-button/?guccounter=1&guce_referrer=aHR0cHM6Ly93d3cuYmluZy5jb20v&guce_referrer_sig=AQAAADUWIEk4CGyl8JUBLHUyX3sDMBCsT2890Z76S-cla9VreMjgHQMTR_7jsa_BkYrzrYAsn49rKrp7en-esRfBSHJEpblQMMjZKYsRbUOfzAIi62S7ut9E-Ee0pChNVgEK41jgQZl640BKyygj-829uC_sZtmMBA4FZhNzNI-PjjHp [Accessed 1 August 2022].

King, D.A. and Saldarriaga, J.F., (2017) 'Access to taxicabs for unbanked households: An exploratory analysis in New York City', *Journal of Public Transportation*, 20(1), pp. 1–19. doi:10.5038/2375-0901.20.1.1

Koffman, D., (2016) 'Transportation network companies and paratransit: Issues and opportunities', *Transport and Sustainability*, 8, pp. 377–390. doi:10.1108/S2044-994120160000008018

Leisy, C.A., (2019) *Transportation network companies and taxis: The case of Seattle*. Routledge, ISBN 9780367729653

Mallinson, K., (2015) 'Smartphone revolution: Technology patenting and licensing fosters innovation, market entry, and exceptional growth', *IEEE Consumer Electronics Magazine*, 4(2), pp. 60–66. doi:10.1109/MCE.2015.2392954.

Mason, D.P. and Menard, M., (2021) *The impact of ride hail services on the accessibility of nonprofit services*, NITC-RR-1357. Portland, OR: Transportation Research and Education Center (TREC).

ORR, (2022) Office of Rail and Road Regulation (UK), Monitoring the impact of, and response to, open access 2022 Update, 28 April 2022. Available at: https://www.orr.gov.uk/sites/default/files/2022-04/open-access-monitoring-report-2022-update.pdf

Reinke, D., (1986) 'Update on taxicab and jitney regulation in San Diego', *Transportation Research Record*, 1103, p. 9.

Rodden, J., (2007) 'Glasgow City Centre 'Nite Zone' Project', *Scottish Transport Applications and Research STAR conference*, Available at: https://starconference.org.uk/star/2007/Jamie_Rodden.pdf

SAN DIEGO MTS, (2020) 'An ordinance providing for the licensing and the regulating of transportation services within the city and county by the adoption of a uniform paratransit ordinance', San Diego Metropolitan Transit System (ed.) Codified ordinance no. 11 (as amended through November 12, 2020).

Schaller, B., (2015) 'Between public and private examining the rise of technology-enabled transportation services', *TRB Special Report 319*, [Online] Available: http://www.schallerconsult.com/rideservices/sharedmobility.htm [Accessed 1 August 2022].

Schaller, B., (2018) 'Second chances, regulation and deregulation of taxi and for-hire ride services', *TR News*, 315, pp. 243–248.

Smeds, E., Robin, E. and McArthur, J., (2020) 'Night-time mobilities and (in)justice in London: Constructing mobile subjects and the politics of difference in policy-making', *Journal of Transport Geography*, 82, doi:10.1016/j.jtrangeo.2019.102569

Stein, E.J. and Head, B.W., (2020) 'Uber in Queensland: From policy fortress to policy change', *Australian Journal of Public Administration*, 79, pp. 462–479. doi:10.1111/1467-8500.12416

Teal, R.F. and Berglund, M., (1987) 'The impacts of taxicab deregulation in the USA', *Journal of Transport Economics and Policy*, 21(1), pp. 37–56. [Online] Available: http://www.jstor.org/stable/20052801 [Accessed 1 August 2022].

Uber BV and others (Appellants) v Aslam and others (Respondents), (2018) EWCA Civ 2748 [2021] UKSC 5 On appeal from: [2018] [Online] Available at: https:// www. supremecourt.uk/cases/docs/uksc-2019-0029-judgment.pdf [Accessed 1 August 2022].

UCLA, (2018) 'More than a gig, a survey of ride-hailing drivers in Los Angeles', *UCLA Institute for Research on Labor and Employment UCLA Labor Center*, [Online] Available at: https://www.labor.ucla.edu/wp-content/uploads/2018/06/Final-Report.-UCLA-More-than-a-Gig.pdf [Accessed 1 August 2022].

Waterhouse, P., (1993) *Analysis of taxicab deregulation and deregulation. Prepared for the International Taxicab Foundation.* Nov 8 1993. Available at: https://www.rank&file.ca/wp-content/uploads/2016/02/Price3.pdf

7 Taxi Company and Driver Perspectives

For the traditional operator, the arrival and proliferation of the transportation network company (TNC) has brought wave upon wave of bad news. The new mode has established a rapid increase in passenger trip numbers, illustrated in Figure 7.1, in the case of New York, from a standing start managing to eclipse the traditional industry within three years of operation.

For the taxi company, the relative stability of the decade to around 2014 saw little change in passenger number, a pattern repeated across many cities. Seasonal variations were apparent, but little variation in total demand by year was observed, nor was any significant effort extended, by the taxi companies, to change the dynamic. Traditional taxi companies could be described as serving the market with only limited interest to create change, effectively a

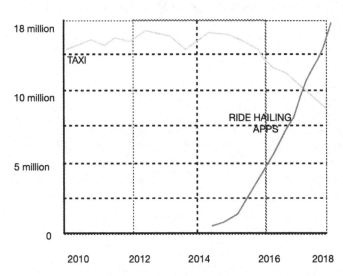

NEW YORK CITY
Monthly Taxi Pick Ups, trend lines

Figure 7.1 Comparative trend lines, pick-up count, taxi and TNC, in New York.
Source: Authors, data: NYC Taxi and Limousine Commission.

DOI: 10.4324/9781003256311-8

cash cow under the Boston Consulting Group's stylisation of business cycles. Comparison across transport industries suggests the cycle was likely to support the continuation of the model toward, and somewhat after, its first point of decline, rather than any form of significant innovation within the trade.

In some instances, efforts had been made to evolve the business, often through targeted sector-specific initiatives, including the 'zTrip' concept rolled out by YellowCab in a number of US cities. While the concept, and others like it, did move towards app use, it appeared more a rebranding effort, in much the same way that the traditional aviation industry had seen the growth of an 'Airline Within an Airline' (AWA) concept (Heiets et al., 2021), as a response to low-cost carriers entry to the market. Examples of the AWA concept include the British Airways subsidiary companies BA Connect, GoFly, and BA CitiFlyer, amongst others (Pearson and Merkert, 2014).

Rebranding of taxi companies was also seen as an effort to draw the focus away from the industry's traditional taxi image, a move accelerated to combat the stylisation of 'big-taxi', a term applied with negative connotations against the traditional trade. Other rebranding exercises were seen in the period, including those championed by taxi app companies seeking to expand app-based bookings, including Flywheel, an app concentrated in the US on west coast cities. European examples include the FreeNow app, 'mobility' app, an updated iteration of earlier apps such as Hailo, with the addition of cross modal functionality, also referred to as 'co-modality' (Biosca et al., 2013; de Stasio et al., 2011; Ronald et al., 2016). In China, Huawei's Petal 'mobility' app is linked to Shouqi Limousine & Chauffeur, UCAR, Sunshine Mobility, and T3 Mobility, illustrating the links between FHV modes and the emergence of a multi-modal technology concept that has become known as mobility as a service (MaaS). MaaS incorporates and expands on the emerging app technologies to achieve *'modal efficiency'*, including those in the taxi industry (Wong et al., 2020), described as a *'mobility intermediary'* in Lyons et al. (2019). The extent to which TNCs may choose to be categorised as MaaS services appears unclear (Schweiger, 2018), though many of their services, and newly introduced categories allied to transit and accessibility, would appear to fall within this category.

Trip Reallocation versus Trip Growth

The arrival of TNCs not only created an impetus for change but also began to expose some of the differences in direction, aims, and market orthodoxies present. The taxi market, prior to TNCs, had been largely assumed static. Any expansion in supply had, at best, been allied to (vaguely) linear relationships between taxi use, population size, and in some instances, visitor populations. Under these assumptions, the arrival of a new operator would reallocate a slice of the total taxi market, pie, leaving the original operator with a lesser amount, and exclude the possibility of either transport market growth or trip diversion delivering a market split more favourable to the FHV market.

The fear being highlighted, and somewhat dispelled by Schaller (2015) who notes opposition, to reform, from medallion owners in the New York market, fearing '*that issuance of new medallions would reduce their daily earnings, assuming a fixed pie of taxi demand*'. Schaller continues (ibid.) to rebut the fear with the observation that... '*when New York City issued additional licenses in the 1990s, driver incomes were little impacted and medallion values rose*'. The observation allows for the possibility of an alternative to the fixed pie theory.

In the event, statistics suggest that both points of view may have been justified. Effectively that the total market for FHV services has increased, a bulk of which growth is attributable to the TNC entrants, at the same time that the overall numbers of trips made by traditional modes had fallen. Effectively that the taxi operator has seen their predicted losses occur, while the predictions of overall market gains allied to the new entrants have also been achieved (Berger et al., 2018).

Taxi Companies, Busy Doing Not Enough

From the taxi company perspective, the fear/threat of a new market entrant was, initially at least, reduced by a view that existing taxi regulations would be sufficient to limit their impact. Two refrains appear common in the early days of app competition, the first that the taxi companies were investing in their own apps, and second that the regulated environment limited or prevented market entry by TNCs.

In both instances, the companies' views appeared to reflect some of the realities of the time. Taxi apps had emerged, even predating some of the TNCs, offered by commercial app suppliers, such as Taxi Magic in the USA, MyTaxi and Hailo in the EU, and their successor multi-nationals, including Gett and FreeNow. The app market appeared split between a small number of very large app providers, alongside a large number of small apps, including 'white label apps'. Early apps, as well as many developed since, remained limited in functionality, while the ownership models, typically separating app from operator, was to create a significant barrier to their success. That said, the argument that the taxi company had an app was persuasive and often became a standard response to questions whether the taxi industry was doing enough.

Not that the field was without innovation, with regional and international taxi apps emerging as the TNC market became an apparent success. Early taxi apps were followed by more advanced versions that included TaxiEU, a successful German venture, Gett, a joint Israeli and, latterly, UK-based app, and FreeNow, while others, notably the International Road Union vision of a multinational taxi app "Up Top", were rapidly scaled back. The IRU concept was repositioned as a Global Taxi Service Quality Network, later the Global Taxi Network (GTN), likely as a result of data sharing and app access issues that would plague taxi app entrants of the time. The GTN was eventually downgraded to a certification system in 2015, rather than the interconnected app network originally envisaged (Taxi Times, 2014).

Image 7.1 London taxi advertisement for Taxi App 'Gett', appearing alongside the taxi company logo.
Source: Authors.

Taxi companies also appeared to rely, heavily, on the effectiveness of local regulation as a protection against new entrants muscling-in on their turf. Many, if not most, authorities had enacted ordinances around the provision of taxis in their cities. The exact nature differed, albeit only slightly, between locations, with UK and EU regulations often defined against national standards, applied locally. In Scotland, this included the Civic Government (Scotland) Act 1982 and the Transport Act 1985 across England and Wales. In each instance, the local (municipal) authority was likely to be designated as the licensing agency, responsible for taxi regulation, with similar patterns across many other European locations.

As most urban locations applied quantity controls at the time, effectively a limit in the number of taxis that may operate, the market could have been seen as closed to new entrants. The strength of this reliance is somewhat challenged by the existence of less stringently controlled PHVs and limousines but stood valid, on the surface, as a barrier to new taxis entering the market.

Regulatory Reassurance in Question

The reassurance of regulation as a safeguard appeared, frequently, as a defence of the standing industry. Effectively that the regulatory authorities would support a traditional industry by excluding new, unlicensed, operations. Many authorities did just that, particularly in the US, where a spate of 'cease and desist' notices were handed down, by the regulators, to TNC vehicles considered to be operating illegally.

Regulatory enforcement activities increased as the TNCs themselves moved from the engagement of black car services, where there was a (slight) justification that vehicles were 'licensed', to the non-professional vehicles typified by Lyft and others, the majority of which operated outside traditional licensing boundaries. The relative position of these services vis-à-vis the regulated environment would continue to be critical, in the case of the TNCs creating the accusation of regulated ambiguity, whether or not such ambiguity existed.

For the taxi operator, the regulator's initial reaction, being the enforcement of regulations through cease-and-desist notices, is likely to have provided a level of reassurance. The regulator had, at least initially, responded in favour of the traditional industry, though the constant challenges to the regulators' authority would eventually lead to a change in approach and perception. Public opinion was also important here, as the taxi operators and regulators could now be painted as colluding with the industry – against the TNC. In the meantime, public demand continued for the new technologies, still not fully embraced by the incumbent taxi, to create an atmosphere set against the status quo. The traditional industry could now be stylised as opposing advancement, while the regulator could be painted as in the enthral to the traditional industry.

Continued opposition to the new entrant resulted in multiple and many city hearings, fines, and citations. At each hearing, the arguments for, and against, TNCs were aired, becoming rehearsed and detailed on the part of the TNC, with no let-up in the determination of the larger TNCs to expand their services. The public platform having been created by the hearings became politicised, with voting council members switching towards the new entrant, often in response to the public pressures, as well as professional lobbying efforts depleting resources on all sides. The continued arguments would eventually prove massively counterproductive to the traditional taxi industry, as public opposition to their position became apparent.

Taxi Company Responses to TNC Expansion

Having painted itself into a corner, the traditional taxi industry had little left with which to oppose the expansion of TNCs. The taxi would, eventually, be seen to respond in the market; as the TNC app increased in popularity, so the need for a taxi equivalent became apparent.

TNC expansion was seen on at least two fronts, the increasing number of cities in which TNCs were available and a (rapid) increase in the number of categories offered on their app. Uber and Lyft between them began offering many dozens of service variants packaged on the single storefront(s), with both large US apps venturing further to link food delivery, with parcels and various novelty delivery options to their platform.

For their part, traditional taxis began to launch and market their own apps more seriously. Some particular responses are of note, with the move of the San Francisco Desoto and Luxor taxi fleets to branding and dispatch as Flywheel a good example, taking hold in the California city from 2015. A similar link-up, effectively a buy-out of the London Radio Taxis fleet by the taxi app, Gett, saw the branding and TNC-like dispatch of an existing fleet in London and its further expansion to other cities in the UK.

While many of the same difficulties persisted, that the taxi fleet would only partially fall within the app-oriented market, continuing a reliance on non-app engagements. This lessened the significance of the app itself to overall income. Equally, while all of the market could benefit, not all would. Taxi operators outside the larger companies, sometimes called street taxis, and some within distanced themselves from the app market, typically remaining off-circuit and concentrated on street hail and taxi stand markets, though the step change is likely to have had a positive impact on the taxi market more generally, creating an opening for TNC market passengers to look more favourably on the taxi alternatives.

Despite the advances in taxi app functionality (Harding et al., 2016), the total uptake of taxi, as opposed to TNC, bookings appeared stubbornly low, with relative market shares declining for the taxi mode.

For their part, private hire vehicles were affected slightly differently, with distinct differences between locations where the TNC companies had been obliged to register as PHV companies, notably the UK and Ireland. Additional resilience could be seen in the Irish market having been one of the earliest countries to deregulate in the current round of reforms, the third wave. It is likely that the market shock effects of deregulation in Ireland, following the 2000 reform of the taxi market, prepared the industry well for the onset of TNC-style services (Koehler, 2004). The Irish market is also notable from the establishment of government-backed hardship fund, though ultimately little called upon (Gorecki, 2017; Weir, 2019); the fund established a get-out route for some in the industry, while the same reforms also highlighted the link between market structure, the presence of *de facto* monopolies in the market, and medallion values.

Medallion Values

While the relative (dis)benefits of the third wave of regulatory reform remain in discussion and will often reflect the 'side' from which they are viewed, it is demonstrably the case that market change has impacted on the relative values of the traditional trade and its competitors. For the taxi industry, this is most easily illustrated through medallion values.

The medallion, also referred to as a taxi plate, license, or certificate (of convenience and necessity), conveys its holder/its holder's vehicle(s), the right to operate as taxis. In most instances, the medallion is a permit issued by and maintained under the authority of the (taxi) licensing agency and inferring specific operating rights and requirements. In recent years, these rights have become associated with the right to ply-for-hire as a cruising taxi and accept hailed ride engagement. In a majority of locations, this specific right is reserved for licensed taxis only, effectively those holding the 'medallion'.

From its early incarnations, the medallion has been charged for, at a cost associated with its administration, i.e. how much it costs the authority to issue it. Licence fees may be ongoing, for example for the renewal of the medallion over time, and would typically be borne by the operator. Medallion value differs from administrative cost, however, insofar as the medallion has become a tradable asset in its own right in some key locations. Indeed, in many locations, legitimate and grey markets have emerged to allow the transfer of a licence between sellers and purchasers. In more restrictive markets, where direct trading is banned or discouraged, medallion transfer can occur through the sale of the taxi company (with medallions). Specific taxi medallion financing companies have emerged, as a method of mortgaging the asset – the medallion, though these companies have experienced significant impacts too, as the market changes question some of the certainties of the medallion market (Wyman, 2013).

In some cities, the regulator receives an income, typically in the form of a fee, from each medallion issued or transferred. In Chicago, the regulatory agency, the Department of Business Affairs and Consumer Protection, receives a medallion transfer fee levied on each such exchange, while New York has traditionally held a new medallion auction selling medallions at their market value, rather than their administrative cost. The effective monopolies created by a closed number of licences is also referred to in a number of texts (Evans, 1993; Çetin et al., 2013). The monopoly encouraged upward pressures on medallion values, with the highest value reported as $1.3million (Harnett, 2018), falling to a low reported in May 2021 of $79,106, a mere 6% of its highest value (Daus, 2022). Across most cities, TNC entry could be seen to create a rapid decline in medallion values, crashing to new lows on news

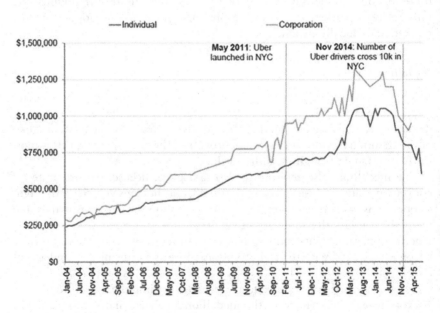

Figure 7.2 Individual and corporate medallion prices in New York.
Source: NYC Taxi and Limousine Commission.

of increasing legitimacy amongst TNC operators, serving a seemingly lethal blow to the traditional distribution and sales of medallions (see Figure 7.2).

Taxi Driver Responses

For their part, the taxi driver was probably feeling the most vulnerable of the market participants. Much of the traditional industry market share was reported as being lost to the TNC competitor, with quite a lot of empirical evidence to support this supposition. Driver self-interest began to move away from any corporate interest, with a clear separation of behaviours both appropriate and followed through the various waves of deregulation.

For a more detailed analysis, it is worth looking at the most recent, third wave of deregulation, as this includes the wide-scale uptake of TNC services and is likely to be the most severe. At this point, a measurable loss of passengers was being met with an increasing reduction in the cap on vehicle numbers. The number of passengers per vehicle was declining, giving some justification to the Mundy model of the slice of the pie available to the taxi industry and to the individual driver. In such circumstances, being the observed and visible decline in per-vehicle passengers, the logical response for a driver would be to maximise the amount of income on each occasion. This effectively rules out any industry initiatives to compete on price and puts a pressure on the regulatory authorities to increase fares in line with declining incomes. Indeed, a number of authorities did exactly that, with a driver earnings element built into the traditional cost indices being applied to fares, the effect of the decline was to put fares up.

Operators, vehicle owners, and lease companies would be likely to see a decline in vehicle profitability; with less money left over to support new vehicle purchase, or even expensive maintenance, the fleets would be likely to decline in quality and increase in vehicle age. The result being the start of a divisive downward spiral, indeed one that led to taxi driver protests, go-slows, and in some instances, violent demonstrations: none of which played well in the public eye and probably worked against the long-term interest of the industry.

Unrest was accompanied by an exodus of drivers from the industry, speeded up by the additional burdens of the Covid pandemic to result in a lack of drivers as demand returned, and the opportunity, taken up by some of the larger TNCs, to take further customers away, despite some actions to link taxi fleets to the TNCs' own platforms, the success of which has not yet been gauged.

Covid and Economic Challenges

In addition to the review of regulatory reform, the discussion of the changing FHV industry needs to also address wider external economic and societal changes that have and continue to impact on the taxi market.

The onset of the Covid pandemic impacted on the taxi industry significantly at a time of major change in progress as a result of the third wave of deregulation and the rapid uptake of TNC services. The pandemic itself reduced demand across all FHV modes, largely as a result of enforced lockdowns and a change in the patterns of work affecting the number of commute and business trips. Initial lockdowns, and a number of further restrictions, prohibited all but essential trips for a period of close to two years, with some variation between countries. The period from around March 2000 enforced stay-at-home orders with the result that the travel industry became unable to support itself on a commercial basis. The effects impacted across all modes, with similar declines in trip numbers to mere fractions of their original levels.

For their part, the taxi industry, comprising mainly self-employed drivers, was badly placed to survive, with many in the industry taking the opportunity to retire or seek alternative employment. In some locations, including Scotland, government intervention was provided in the form of financial support, though only limited support was provided to self-employed people.

The removal of travel restrictions occurred from 2021 and into 2022, being the effective removal of stay-at-home orders, though the interim period between lockdown and reopening had allowed, or required, a significant move to working from home practices, which continued beyond the end of lockdown and remains visible at the time of writing. The reduced occurrence of a regular commuting trip continues to affect the absolute demand for travel, with continuing readjustment of public transport as a result.

For its part, the FHV industry appears to have been surprised by the level of demand returning. Alongside a number of other travel modes, the taxi market had lost a significant proportion of its drivers, while those that remain were in large demand. The shortage of drivers complicates the market further and leads to an entente between the taxi and its TNC competitors. The effective truce was further added to be an apparent desire to work together to meet demand. The outcome, at the time of writing, being a formal link between the largest US TNCs and app-based taxi dispatch, making the taxi mode available as a choice to intending TNC app passengers. Though this model had been tested, without particular success, in limited locations before, the current iteration has the potential to be more successful, likely per force, as a result of the overall shortage of drivers across the whole industry.

A final issue, that might yet impact and derail the shaky recovery, is the global economic declines that have followed from the invasion of Ukraine, affecting a wide sweep of consumer costs and more localised economic drivers, including BREXIT as affecting the UK, amongst others. The currently observed high fuel cost is an immediate indicator, amongst many other consumer elements. The effect of high inflation rates at the time of writing on driver wage is difficult to estimate and compare.

References

Berger, T., Chen, C. and Frey, C.B., (2018) 'Drivers of disruption? Estimating the Uber effect', *European Economic Review*, 110, pp.197–210. doi:10.1016/j.euroecorev.2018.05.006.

Biosca, O., Ulied, A., Caramanico, G., Bielefeldt, C., Calvet, M., Carreras, B., ... Franchi, L. (2013) *Compass: Optimised co-modal passenger transport from reducing carbon emissions: Handbook of ICT solutions for improving co-modality in passenger transport*, Edinburgh: European Commission

Çetin, T. and Eryigit, K.Y., (2013) 'The economic effects of government regulation: Evidence from the New York taxicab market', *In Transport Policy*, 25, pp. 169–177. ISSN 0967-070X, doi:10.1016/j.tranpol.2012.11.011.

Daus, M., (2022) 'Rising medallions could be good news for All NYC transportation', *Chauffer Driven*, 10(8), p. 26.

de Stasio, C., Fiorello, D. and Maffii, S., (2011) 'Public transport accessibility through co-modality: Are interconnectivity indicators good enough?', *Research in Transportation Business & Management*, 2, pp. 48–56. ISSN 2210-5395, doi:10.1016/j.rtbm.2011.07.003

Evans, A.W., (1993) 'On monopoly rent: Reply', *Land Economics*, 69, pp. 111–112.

Gorecki, Paul K., (2017) 'Competition and vested interests in taxis in Ireland: A tale of two statutory instruments', *Transportation Research Part A: Policy and Practice*, 101, pp. 228–237. ISSN 0965-8564, doi:10.1016/j.tra.2017.04.024

Harding, S., Kandlikar, M. and Gulati, S., (2016) 'Taxi apps, regulation, and the market for taxi journeys', *Transportation Research Part A: Policy and Practice*, 88, pp. 15–25, ISSN 0965-8564, doi:10.1016/j.tra.2016.03.009.

Harnett, S., (2018) 'Cities made millions selling taxi medallions, now drivers are paying the price', All Things Considered, NPR.com, October 15, 20184:28 PM ET. Available at: https://www.npr.org/2018/10/15/656595597/cities-made-millions-selling-taxi-medallions-now-drivers-are-paying-the-price

Heiets, I., Oleshko, T. and Leshchinsky, O., (2021) 'Airline-within-Airline business model and strategy: Case study of Qantas Group', *Transportation Research Procedia*, 56, pp. 96–109. ISSN 2352-1465, doi:10.1016/j.trpro.2021.09.012

Koehler, B., (2004) 'Regulating supply in taxi markets', *City University Department of Economics*. Available at: https://citeseerx.ist.psu.edu/viewdoc/download?doi=10.1.1.732.2814&rep=rep1&type=pdf

Lyons, G., Hammond, P. and Mackay, K. (2019) 'The importance of user perspective in the evolution of MaaS', *Transportation Research Part A: Policy and Practice*, 121, pp. 22–36. ISSN 0965-8564, doi:10.1016/j.tra.2018.12.010

Pearson, J. and Merkert, R., (2014) 'Airlines-within-airlines: A business model moving East', *Journal of Air Transport Management*, 38, pp. 21–26, ISSN 0969-6997, doi:10.1016/j.jairtraman.2013.12.014

Ronald, N., Yang, J. and Thompson, R.G., (2016) 'Exploring co-modality using on-demand transport systems', *Transportation Research Procedia*, 12, pp. 203–212, ISSN 2352-1465, doi:10.1016/j.trpro.2016.02.059

Schaller, B., (2015) 'Between public and private examining the rise of technology-enabled transportation services', *TRB Special Report 319*, [Online] Available at: http://www.schallerconsult.com/rideservices/sharedmobility.htm [Accessed 1 August 2022].

Schweiger, C., (2018) 'Improved mobility through blurred lines', *Journal of Public Transportation*, 21(1) pp. 60–66.

Taxi Times, (2014) 'IRU launches worldwide certification for apps', *Taxi Times*, 13 November 2014. Available at: https://www.taxi-times.com/iru-launches-worldwide-certification-for-apps/

Weir, S., (2019) 'The liberalisation of taxi policy: Capture and recapture?', *Administration*, 67(2), pp. 113–135. doi:10.2478/admin-2019-0016

Wyman, K.M., (2013) 'Problematic private property: the case of New York taxicab medallions', *Yale Journal on Regulation*, 30, p. 125. Available at: https://openyls.law.yale.edu/bitstream/handle/20.500.13051/8178/05_30YaleJonReg125_2013_.pdf

Wong, Y.Z., Hensher, D. and Mulley, C., (2020) 'Mobility as a service (MaaS): Charting a future context', *Transportation Research Part A: Policy and Practice*, 131, pp. 5–19, ISSN 0965-8564, doi:10.1016/j.tra.2019.09.030

8 Regulator Perspectives

The Role of the Regulator

In previous chapters, we have sought to establish the historical context of the for hire vehicle (FHV), its patterns of use, and legislative structure(s). In this chapter, we address the practical, political, and operational aspects of regulation and the role of the regulator. It is notable that the precise terminology applied to the role will differ, as will the title and legal status of the regulator themselves. For clarity, we define a regulator as an official, government, or agency role intended to design, develop, enact, and enforce distinct controls to ensure the correct operation of (the taxi industry), in providing appropriate services within a defined geography. The role is frequently associated with a local government and will therefore include a political element, as may include the need for local government committee approvals, statute, and/or area-based codification.

While an element of regulatory control is almost universal across the FHV industry,[1] the extent to which this control is the remit of a taxi regulator can differ. The role of the regulator is based on and reflects both the perceived and real need for such regulation. The regulator's role can also be influenced by the existing administrative structure of its location, the relative power and influence of the market participants, as well as the extent to which wider government(s) seek to permit free markets, regulated competition, or control.

Against this backdrop, regulatory agencies can face regular and repeated challenges to their authority, even to their existence. Such challenges range from taxi customers seeking adjudication over fares and service; from taxi companies who may disagree with the cost or application of rules; and from the external market, most recently new market entrants seeking access to a previously controlled market. The result is a differing regulation across a variety of FHV vehicles well beyond the definition of an economic structure to one that fills in policy goals and gaps; political and social aspirations, which can differ; and an inherent conflict, between many, sometimes all, players, to garner maximum benefits, all in the public interest, of course.

In some cities, the agency of the regulator themselves may also be uncertain; as a part of an administration, the agency would be bound by the (local

DOI: 10.4324/9781003256311-9

and political) views of the city council or administrative structure within which it sits. Add to this the combination of lobbying and a rapidly changing market, the regulator's role is hardly simple.

Regulatory Context

Despite the myriad challenges very lightly touched on above, regulatory practices and its regulators appear to have existed with long periods of stability. Such stability is challenged only occasionally, often by a period of frenetic activity that may follow changes in other forms of regulation, changes in technologies, and/or changes in supply-side operations sometimes stylised as reforms.

A period of frenetic activity within the regulation of taxis is visible in the US in the 1980s, occurring, and possibly influenced by parallel deregulation of the airline industry prompted by the 1978 Airline Deregulation Act. The taxi market is affected by a wider emphasis on free market economic principles and subsequent deregulations. The period of the early 1980s witnessed a series of deregulations and privatisations, giving rise to the label of a deregulatory movement, seen both in North America and Europe, with wide-scale movement away from nationalised industries across telecommunications, utilities, power, and transportation, discussed in the preceding chapters. Taxi regulations began to diverge in this period between the US and comparable European locations, the same pressures not translating into wide-scale reform in the EU market, though some examples of a looser regulatory framework did follow in Europe over the same time period, not least the growth of the lesser regulated FHV market, being able to compete openly on price and facing lower barriers to entry in some EU states.

For its part, the North American taxi market has received its fair share of criticism. Service complaints were visible across all types of passengers and businesses in the US, aimed both at the taxi companies and their regulators. Cities were forced to acknowledge and address the complaints, with many concluding that the issues arose from a lack of effective regulation, effectively that the system then in place was not working. The period that followed from the early 1980s included a series of regulatory reforms, typically derestriction and deregulation (Teal and Berglund, 1987), derestriction focused on the (restricted) number of vehicles, deregulation on the other elements of quality and economic control. It is notable that the reforms of the 1980s were largely short-lived with deregulation being followed in many cities by re-regulation over the remaining decade.

The period directly following was typified by relative calm, stable regulation, over which time regulatory practices became established and entrenched as the, now stable, market allowed for a consistency in regulation. As regulatory functions became defined (once again), the city councils reallocated regulatory authority to departments, though with little consistency between locations. Regulator roles were allocated, in the USA, to a mix of police, business standards, licensing, and administrative affairs departments, amongst others, though rarely to actual transport departments, with the result that the taxi service, clearly a form of transport, would almost always be controlled separately to more mainstream transport.[2]

The period of relative stability in the USA between the mid-1980s and the 2010s was next interrupted from around 2012 largely as a result of the emergence of transportation network companies (TNCs) and subsequent challenges associated therewith.

Regulator Roles

The period of regulatory stability provides a focus for 'ordinary activity'. Regulator roles became apparent and practiced, though rarely easy. Regulators could now establish their relationships across the FHV market, defining regulation and enforcement to both the taxi and its derivative limousine and private car segments. Regulation became a local activity, largely defined at city and district authority levels, upholding the principle that a city regulator would be better placed to establish what worked in their location for locally based suppliers and customers than a state or national one. This local approach would become a more significant issue as national and multi-national operators were to follow. Localisation also created challenges to a consistent national or federal process, though some countries were able to determine legislative and regulatory norms, while others, including the US, saw the development of regulator associations. Equivalent structures can be seen in the UK, using the example of Scotland where taxi licensing regulations are defined in national law, the Civic Government (Scotland) Act 1982, but applied through city regulators. Effectively, the Scottish Government defines the frameworks within which the local authorities may operate.

Additional complications can of course arise where trips cross regulatory boundaries, an instance common in locations with larger metropolitan areas comprising multiple administrative jurisdictions, while most authorities facing boundary issues have established methods for their operation.

Semantic definitions may also complicate application, and analysis, of regulation, particularly for private hire (non-taxi) trips, which can include a range of differing service types, definitions and regulations that include: charter, sightseeing, fixed route, and non-emergency medical transportation uses. Which vehicles can and are regulated are dictated by the categorisation into which they fit. Differing basic interpretations affect the ability of any one view to be taken, while actually legislated differences between locations, including neighbouring authorities, complicate the situation still further.

Distinctions have also emerged between agencies by vehicle type, with some cities separating taxis from limousines, with an increasing trend in the USA for TNCs to be regulated completely separately from other forms of FHV, including in some instances at a differing administrative/geographical level. An example is California, where taxis remain regulated at a city or regional level, TNCs at a state level, by the California Public Utilities Commission (CPUC).

State boundaries also impact on regulation, with the potential for significantly different regulations one side of the state line compared to the other. The same conflict is seen in Canada between provinces, and the UK across devolved government nations. In the US instance, inter-state transportation follows significantly different and separate licensing to that within a city's boundaries.

In addition, in recent years, the complex nature of taxi regulation has become an issue for the regulatory organisations for whom the taxi was not a core element. Examples include police departments and business bureaux were allocated the taxi regulation portfolio, despite the limited or tangential nature of their link to taxis. Police departments have been seen to agitate that more traditional policing responsibilities should take priority, effectively that taxi regulatory responsibilities were removing officers from doing 'actual police work'. Issues of resourcing and financing resulted in some instances where taxi regulation fell down a list of priorities, with the result that taxi regulation could appear the poor relation of the department. In some larger cities, such as Boston USA, police officers are required to develop skills not typically associated with police work, including vehicle safety/marking inspections, vehicle route checks, taxicab metre inspections, complaints handling, and adjudication, over and above standard practice.

The net effect of the period of stability is that of increasing complexity in regulations, including the development of differences between the regulations of neighbouring authorities and a lack of transparency in some instances. Controls applied in support of regulations moved away from free-market principles to that of regulated competition, while operational measurements and consistent need to account for changes in market conditions required of the market type would often be overlooked. Complex models measuring unmet demand and cost indices applied to economic regulations would emerge and be applied to different levels of success, often creating rancour amongst the trade and public alike.

Further complexities have also emerged as the trade began to suffer from declining wages compared to its alternatives, not least as a result of the limited application of a measured approach to regulated competition. Regulators also failed to account for population changes, as driver communities would be associated, in the USA, with particular demographics, each with the potential for internal dispute, while new market entrants' business models built on a rapid turnover of staff, aka churn, and dependent on a continued supply of drivers willing to enter the market. Most recent externalities include the effect of Covid on the supply and use of taxis. The pandemic saw both a rapid reduction of demand over its lockdown periods; loss of drivers, including many leaving the industry to retire or take up alternative employment; and the subsequent, consequent, inability of the market to resize upwards as demand returned. The latter element, an inability to increase supply, has a greater impact on the supply of taxis than on TNCs, as the new entrants are, generally, able to increase fares to reflect excess levels of demand, whereas the traditional industry is not. In short, the newer TNC market was and remains better placed to scale its offering compared to the taxi market, hastening the loss of market share to the TNC.

Regulatory Politics

Having established the evolution and development of a regulatory structure, it is also appropriate to address and observe its politics. While each city may reflect differences of opinion, it is also notable that many factors remain the same. Taxi regulations are generally left outside the sphere of transportation, and apply, or are justified, on the basis of public protection. That the market would not deliver an optimal solution operating in the public interest, free of control. The concept of regulated competition follows that the regulator estimates and imposes regulations that approximate the free market in its absence. The justification is fraught with complexity, not least that the open operation of the market unencumbered is unlikely, thus denying the opportunity to establish a realistic baseline, and that any and all attempts to ensure free-market equivalent operations are open to critique and pressure.

For many years, that pressure was manifest from the taxi community itself. The industry argues in its interest at a local level, as a commercial, unsubsidised form of transport effectively competing with public transport modes in receipt of significant subsidies.[3,4] Local public transport would often be given preferential treatment, including in the allocation of road space and priority measures, while being seen to offer a public service, compared to the taxi private and commercial operation. For their part, city councils and council members would typically face pressures from the public in respect of the quality, price, and competence of the typical taxi, despite many of these areas falling within the competence of the city's own department, effectively applying a continual pressure on the licensing authority, to improve their own performance, and making the role of the regulator a relatively hapless task.

The arrival of TNCs further exacerbated the potential for conflict at a city level. The TNC, as distinct from its app, represented a differing approach to FHV transport, while offering a product that was, to all extents and purposes, the same. These distinctions, both between the TNC and an app, and between taxis and TNCs, would become a critical issue in the development of the mode and its regulation, as would the conclusion that TNCs and taxis offered highly similar services in the eyes of the public. Several aspects demand attention and have followed over time.

Early forays by the taxi industry into the app market lagged significantly behind other early transport apps and may reasonably be judged to represent slow, late, and basic applications, often restricted to electronic phone directories. In contrast, once started, TNC companies moved quickly, without regard for, and often without knowledge of, the regulatory environment into which they were entering. The TNC represented a nimble and formidable opponent and would often appear aggressive compared to the pedestrian nature of the taxi company. Critically also, the TNC was not limited in any traditional model of physical location; larger companies rapidly adopted a multi-location, cross state, and international corporate structure badly suited to the city and local administration models applied to the taxi industry, while rapidly garnering a following amongst the public where speed of response, a perception of lower fare, and benefits of multi-city use became very popular. The ability of the new entrant to call on the support of a rapidly growing favourable user base would stand the companies in a position of strength and provide a strong bargaining tool in licensing committees deciding on their rights, or otherwise, to operate.

Current and Future Development, Lessons, and Forecasts

The period since 2012 has seen a significant increase in regulatory activity, including regulatory reform. The period has been typified by challenges to regulation, and a rebalancing of the taxi market broadly to accommodate the presence of TNCs, whether with or without agreement from traditional quarters. The rebalancing has not yet reached a conclusion and may be said to remain without market equilibrium. The period of, and since, the Covid pandemic is likely to vary significantly from the trajectory visible prior thereto. Some cities have launched significant updates to their regulations, on a par with the scales of changes last seen in the 1980s, including Los Angeles, passing sweeping changes in February 2022, and broadly adopting an open market system, to replace the earlier franchise operation in force in the city and County of Los Angeles.[5]

The rebalancing period had been approached, initially, by the regulatory community seeking to prevent the operation of TNCs. The new market segment fell outside the traditional definitions of market control and had made it apparent, to the regulatory community, that they would seek to operate in an area of regulatory ambiguity. The larger companies argued that their activities were related to the provision of technology – the platform, rather than the transport services it facilitated. The argument was tested at numerous points in courts in most jurisdictions, with significant gains, wins, and losses throughout the rebalancing period.

For their part, the North American regulators association, the IATR, produced static arguments opposing the entry of TNCs, a range of model regulations, intended to be adopted and thus give a united face to the regulation of the industry, and a resource base reporting on and reviewing the previous periods of (relative) stability. Early regulator responses, including notices to cease and desist, were mainly offered at a local city level; and the issuance of operating fines, to drivers, was visibly in breach of city codes. The actions were broadly unsuccessful, highlighting the contradictions in scale between the local regulator and the multi-national corporation, who would frequently cover any fines or driver citation costs, while also exposing the inadequate nature of such fines in offering a deterrent.

The taxi companies were also represented, in the USA, by their own trade group: the Taxicab Paratransit Limousine Association[6] (TPLA). The TPLA had emerged as a trade group on the back of the period of stability, showcasing vehicles, dispatch equipment, and an annual trade show. The group had also developed its own set of advisory notes, again reflecting the previous era, in support of locally controlled taxi companies as a lobby group supports regulatory requirements. Both groups, the TPLA and IATR, appear to have been caught off-guard as the regulatory implications of the TNCs began to be seen and recognised. The industry appeared content that their regulations could withstand and respond to the new entrant, while the regulators' initial approach retained local primacy, albeit with limited effect. Later responses would move from localised to state and federal government levels in the USA, with similar escalation in Canada and European countries.

The passage of time throughout the rebalancing period appears to have done little to reduce rhetoric and has led to a greater escalation of position and outcome. Initial localised efforts to maintain a stable market balance by regulators have been replaced by more significant actions at the regional level and across a wider number of regulatory aspects. Having agreed to an initial trial period, Transport for London (TfL) took the decision to oppose the renewal of an Uber licence on the grounds that the company did not meet its 'fit and proper person' requirement. TNC drivers in the UK filed for and won the right to be treated as employees, while the European Court of Justice determined Uber was indeed a transportation company, undermining the TNC's argument that any regulation of the company should relate to the technology it provided. In 2022, a consortium of investigative journalists reported on a whistle blower releasing a series of papers 'the Uber papers' revealing TNC corporate approaches to regulators. Each instance addressed an area of regulation but none resulted in a return to the previous status quo. Indeed, as many of the arguments were exercised, contradictions across the wider industry could also be seen.

In one such example, the status of the driver in the USA appeared to be in conflict between segments. With one major exception, taxi drivers in the USA are considered independent contractors, not employees, placing them at odds with the TNC drivers, again with exceptions, classified as employees, and thus with employment rights beyond those of their taxi counterparts. One TNC exception is the status of drivers in California: having been obliged to reclassify drivers as employees in the state, a ballot referendum modified the regulation and re-established contractor status in 2021.

Enforcement

Having answered, or at least identified, the fundamental rights and requirements of regulation, regulators are also faced with the question as to how to enforce them. The issue can be seen from its first bases, how to identify the vehicle – significant for both passenger and enforcement agent alike. In many cases, specific vehicle markings, such as colour, can be defined, with multiple further layers of identification and required information, plate numbers, and passenger information.

Enforcement roles can also fall between agencies or be delegated to outside authorities, most frequently police/law enforcement. This creates issues in and of itself given that taxi regulation will often sit on top of and separate to 'normal' traffic control. This not only requires both additional information and knowledge to be held by the traffic officer but also results in conflicting priorities. Thus, a policing priority to get travelers home form a weekend night out conflicts with a role in enforcing vehicle licences, public safety priorities often felt better served by supporting travelers getting home.

Future Structures

While many challenges remain, not least the ongoing role of regulators at differing levels for differing segments, an unusual peace appears to have broken out. As the pandemic forced a shake out of both sides of the taxi industry, so the roles of each may finally come together.

The traditional medallions/permit market of the taxi has reached what might reasonably be referred to as a market correction. Handfuls, even a majority of licences, have been lost over the pandemic as operators failed, companies lost business, and the excessive costs of medallions in some cities brought the pre-pandemic industry to a head. Taxi companies could not survive in their existing form, while medallion values had become unsustainable to a point of no return. The pandemic resulted in the virtual stoppage of taxi travel in most cities around the world and restarted an industry or reset its core values and valuation.

As of early 2022, with people beginning to travel again, the need for drivers has returned. This time without an old guard, those who had retired, left the industry and got other jobs. Alternatives have made it less appealing to drive for a living, forcing, or at least catalysing, a combination of and joining of forces between the two rivals, the taxi and the TNC. TNCs and taxicab companies agreed to work together in several cities around the world. The new guard of drivers much more content to use apps, a significant departure in the traditional taxi industry, while the app providers themselves have taken steps to coordinate cross-platform API interfaces. Today, the TNC company can easily include the taxi app dispatch as part of their supply as any other driver on their circuit. Gone the hesitant and jittery initial approaches of the taxi app, now there is solid integration between segments. The circumstances appear materially different, both providers are recovering from the pandemic and both need the other to maximise service demand and passenger service levels.

The opportunity appears to apply to all to work towards creating a set of consistent universal standards that a passenger can understand, basic rules of the road no matter where they catch a ride, or who provides it. Not that this is the end of the process. Passengers deserve and need to see the regulatory process work in their interest. The need remains to ensure robust public awareness; fairness in fares and tariffs; and continuing review to ensure how and when independent contractor regulations and/or employee regulations are applied.

Notes

1　The suggestion of universal regulation is likely across operations where taxi services are considered 'legal'. Legal operations refer, in this context, to those whose operating patterns are defined in law and would not prevent an operator of a 'legal' taxi service from being in breach of some of the requirements of their operation. Illegal taxi operations, in contrast, relate to areas of taxi operation that are not sanctioned. Thus, taxibus services operating in South African townships would have been considered illegal. As may have Gypsy cabs operating in some US cities, including Baltimore, amongst others.

2　Notable exceptions include San Diego, where taxi regulation is located within the San Diego Metropolitan Transit System (MTS), though managed separately from transit operations within the MTS. Similar distinct collocation is visible in Los Angeles, under the LA Department of Transportation; in London, as part of Transport for London (TfL), as well as in the case of taxi regulation in Ireland being collocated with Public Transport in the National Transport Authority (NTA), though such examples are the exception, rather than the rule. The fact that a taxi regulatory function is located within the same organisation as Public Transport does not require nor ensure any commonality in planning. Potential collaborative benefits may include street planning, timetable, transport modelling, and/or interchange facilities, amongst others, and are not a necessary outcome of a shared agency.

3　Some locations provide supported services utilising taxis that may include education and NEMT transport. These services are generally let using a competitive tender process.

4　Public transport services may be in receipt of subsidy through a variety of means, with US and North American markets receiving capital and operational grants. Public transport in the UK and EWU is also likely to receive some forms of support, though the mechanism for such support differs by location.

5　The 2022 reforms applied to the City and County of Los Angeles also remove the need for a defined color scheme, as well as simplifying the process for becoming a taxi driver, permitting up-front fares, and requiring data reporting from all operators.

6　Since renamed The Transportation Alliance (TTA), with effect from 2019.

Reference

Teal, R.F. and Berglund, M., (1987) 'The impacts of taxicab deregulation in the USA', *Journal of Transport Economics and Policy*, 21(1), pp. 37–56. [Online] Available at: http://www.jstor.org/stable/20052801 [Accessed 1 August 2022].

9 Perspectives of Transportation Network Companies

While it has been common for the traditional taxi industry to identify many of the negatives faced by the for hire vehicle (FHV) sector to be a result of new app companies, the development of apps and the outcomes of the transport network company (TNC) presence in the market should be distinguished as different. In relation to the technology, the app has brought with it a series of new, advanced, opportunities that have, in global terms, opened up a new level of service not previously available. The potential development and exploitation of the app is/was open to all and widely demonstrated across the provision of wider public transport before becoming widely used in the FHV market. In short, it is not appropriate to tie the technology to the TNC alone, nor should the discussion focus purely on the corporate benefit and/or losses that this link has created.

To develop the argument further, it is important to split the app technology, discussed in its technical aspects in the preceding chapters, from the companies that have, broadly, promoted its uptake. It is also important to highlight that such companies can exist at a variety of levels, spread geographically. The spread of TNCs, as a business model, can appear different by market, with major distinctions in some aspects of corporate style, approach, and effectiveness. In short, the market extends beyond the largest global player(s), despite much of the focus which has appeared to concentrate on one or a small number of such companies. The discussion set out below seeks to extend beyond a critique of any one individual company, though it is also clear that it will, necessarily, draw on examples that are company specific.

TNCs as a Technology Solution

The discussion begins, perhaps logically, with the emergence of the technology, promoted as a solution, and therefore implying the existence of a problem. The global use of the term technology may also be misleading as a number of moving parts and a number of technologies need to align. These are roughly chronologically the emergence and take up of the smartphone; the development, and download of 'apps', as a concept; and their further development into transport solutions, to include, but not be limited to: bookings

DOI: 10.4324/9781003256311-10

platforms and the responses of the various market participants along the way. Important also is the fact that the engagement of taxis, and other FHVs, had, in the early days of app development, remained broadly static for some time, albeit for good reason. Pre-existing uses of the taxi had become, effectively, a baseline against which progress could be compared.

For its part, the smartphone emerged in fits and starts. The current touch-screen generation is often associated with the iPhone, and its Android equivalents, or vice versa to give it its correct chronology, the first touchscreen smartphone likely to be the LG 'Prada' model, properly called the KE850. The HTC Dream is also significant as the first Android phone, announced in 2007; the HTC model incorporated a fold-away keyboard and thus not an example of current smartphone designs, with the first generation iPhone launching the same year. Critical also are the operating systems including iOS (Apple) and Android as the two major systems that have come to dominate the market, as these would host the emerging concept of the smartphone application (App), highly abridged programmes requiring relatively small software memory allocations, of which early versions appear dominated by games. The original App Store, for iOS, carrying 500 such apps was launched in 2007 by Apple. Other operating systems have also emerged, including Huawei Harmony OS, a platform popular across Asia. Harmony OS emerged largely a result of (telecoms) regulatory actions intended to prevent access by Huawei to the Android platform. Other platforms have also emerged, intended to allow earlier phone designs to bridge the gap from traditional to smartphone status, most being unsuccessful. These included the Research In Motion (RIM) Blackberry system, a popular text-oriented intelligent phone widespread amongst businesses prior to the smartphone.

The availability and purposes of apps expanded rapidly, not least in terms of commercial and business uses (Sarwar and Soomro, 2013) to include social media and sales portals. A step change emerged with the integration of GPS location data into the smartphones, the link between GPS location data and app functions opening up significant new opportunities. It is noted that GPS had already been available on mobile phones some time earlier, first by the Benefon 'Esc!' in 1999, while its effectiveness was only fully realised with its integration in apps.

The first app-based use of GPS data appears to have been with the arrival of Google Maps on Android in 2008, the same functions appearing on Google Maps for iOS in 2012, although it is likely that other mapping apps existed prior to this date, including spin-offs and stand-alone satellite navigation systems.

The combination of GPS, mapping, and an increasing interest in location-specific apps, later named location services, would create a base on to which transport and travel concepts could be built.

For their part, the taxi market appeared slow off the mark, with early taxi-specific apps, including Taxi Magic, focused on a minor part of the traditional taxi company business model, discussed in more detail above. The

TNC, in contrast, was dedicated, in its entirety, to the app environment, a fact reinforced by the actions of the regulator in limiting alternative access points. The emergent TNCs developed a digital platform as their primary business product, while the methods of exploiting that platform, including service diversification and innovation, were to follow, with speed in some instances (Hacker, 2018).

The relative speed of development, often a result of commercial necessity, led to reports of the TNC as an aggressive competitor (Matherne and O'Toole, 2017), with larger TNCs described (ibid.) as highly visible '*high-growth start-up[s]*'...'*that received considerable positive and negative attention in the media*'. The media attention contributed to the TNCs' market growth and possibly defined their strategy at the same time. Public attention was drawn, by the press amongst others, to the service (often as a positive), while the same attention-seeking behaviour contributed to the (now negative) views of the traditional industry and its regulators. A further stakeholder group, this time the driver community, was also to enter prominence as the TNCs continued their growth. A position illustrated through the effective commoditisation of drivers by the new entrants: effectively as a part of the capital resource that would benefit, both the company and the drivers themselves, through rapid turn around and continuing jobs or 'gigs'. The TNCs made further use of their 'resource' by opening up their platforms to secondary transportation types, including take-away food delivery, and the expansion of passenger vehicle categories into specific 'comfort' segments, often accompanied by discounting.

A further and major shift followed in July 2012 as a result of intense competition between the US TNCs Uber and Lyft, resulting in the launch of non-professional driver-based services Lyft and UberX, a structure subsequently followed by most other TNCs. The non-professional driver in this context being a private individual, normally in their own car, offering fare-paying passenger trips without seeking licensing as traditional FHV operators or drivers.

Differing Perspectives

The structures and approaches of the TNCs from their traditional FHV counterparts appear to have developed almost from their inception. Most started life from a technology base, with few having been directly involved in the provision of transportation prior to that point. For the nascent TNCs, it would be reasonable to see opportunities as a result of the improved dispatch that their platform could offer to the FHV journey. The TNC could achieve greater benefit from the platform technologies than their traditional competition, who remained focused on lower technology and no-technology trips. This distinction is important as it focuses on the technological nature of the TNC, a fact that could be continued to be argued at the time of writing.

For its part, the early iterations of what became Uber Technologies Inc. appeared focused on a premium market operated in the USA by limousine and Black Car services. The first iterations being named UberCab provided a dispatch to limousines based on the same location aspects of the smartphone app that continue to form a core of their current service offerings. The company ran almost immediately into criticism over the use of the word 'Cab', a term used interchangeably with (hackney) carriage in the taxi trade, and carrying, in the eyes of that trade, implication of a taxi service. In October 2010, the San Francisco Metro Transit Authority and the Public Utilities Commission of California issued a Cease and Desist (C&D) notice to the company, claiming it was operating an unlicensed taxi service. Whether or not as a result, the company did change its name, dropping the term cab but notably continued operating, with the result that it was issued with multiple further C&D notices and fines for non-compliance.

Other app dispatch services present in the US market included Zimride, later to become Lyft, an operating system dispatching to non-professional drivers, originally focused on college shared rides at the University of California Santa Barbara. The presence of shared rides in the emerging TNC market, albeit for profit, was to create a pressure on other TNCs to join suit, with observable 'leap-frogging' in launch dates as the two large US TNCs sought to capture market share.

The move to non-professional drivers also set the scene for multiple critiques, argued, by the larger TNC, as a competitive move required to allow continued survival, as a competitive move to come in line with direct TNC competitors. The TNCs maintained the argument that their role was as the technology provider, their platforms, rather than as the transport provider, the drivers using their platforms. The argument differed sharply from the perceived wisdom of the time, being allied to the taxi company view that they, the taxi company, were definitively involved in the transportation business, while offering many of the same aspects of booking and dispatch also available on the TNC platforms. In many ways, the two 'sides' offered ostensibly the same service, despite one being vehement in its view that it did not provide transport, the other that it did. For the public, the apparent disagreements, and opposing perspectives, did little to diminish from the view that the services offered were effectively the same, with frequent references to the TNCs as being taxi services, both in the press and common culture.

Corporate Ambitions and Funding

In addition to the clear operations differences, sharp differences were also visible in the nature of funding between the traditional industry and the market entrants. TNCs had become adept in highlighting their technological aspects, focusing much of their early media and publicity material on the advantages the technology brought, while focusing their funding efforts heavily on a rapid growth strategy. The focus on expansion suited the larger TNCs well, creating first a national then an international presence in short order in the case of Uber. Within one year of its initial US expansion, Uber had launched in Paris in December 2011; in London and Toronto in 2012; and in Mexico, Taiwan, and India in 2013. Other TNCs remained more focused on national markets, though each sought to expand rapidly within their chosen geographies, in direct contrast to the highly localised city-level presence of most taxi companies.

To achieve their growth, many TNCs relied on venture capital and app-investor funding, which appeared to be readily available to the larger companies despite their apparent lack of significant profit in their early years (Horan, 2017; Bonini and Capizzi, 2019), demonstrating a significant capital in the technological revolution the app would enable and associated benefits from the management structures of the TNCs themselves. Strong management, even the aggressive stance of some TNCs, appeared to attract dividends to an extent that the slow and steady approach of the traditional industry could appear unable to achieve (Lerner and Nanda, 2020).

Corporate ambitions are also significant to the ultimate direction of the industry. TNCs appeared to sit on a continuum between global operations, a rare and limited achievement for some, and solid regional markets, themselves spanning national borders, though to a lesser extent than the identifiable 'global' players. Also apparent, despite common public, and driver, facing apps, the actual delineation between service types and their regulatory definitions differ between countries. Thus, the UberX/UberPop products contain subtle licensing and regulatory differences between countries, complicating their administration, at least from the standpoint of the management company – the TNC. In some locations, individual country operations may be handled by subsidiary companies at a local or regional level, often not only to the benefit of the operator in its localised focus but also in complicating regulatory feedback and challenge: which company and or subsidiary becomes responsible for operations and their assurance and in which jurisdiction.

Overreach may also occur, as some markets become over-saturated by a mix of local, regional, and international apps, leading to the question as to which suits and which will survive in the market. As a counter, a benefit does arise in the single app approach, a global or regional app available across markets without the need for incoming visitors to identify and download multiple apps, often in languages that may not be understood, and sometimes hitting geo-blockers being regional market exclusions applied at the App Store level.

The (perceived) aggressive nature of the App company may also come into play in its success and development. To explore this further, we will start with the epithet itself, whether the TNC really is pushy in its approach and whether, or not, it benefits from the label, whether perceived or demonstrated. For many, an immediate comparator, against which 'behaviour' can be determined, would be the existing taxi and FHV market. The TNC appears to offer much the same service as the taxi and more so when compared to the private hire and limousine markets. TNC companies can appear to have stepped in with little regard for the existing regulatory cultures of the incumbent industry and may even appear to breach licensing codes, as may be seen by a significant backlash and enforcement actions from the various city and licensing authorities in many, if not most, locations. For their part (some), TNCs have argued that their service relies on a technology, rather than the transportation, suggesting in one instance that 'ambiguity' existed insofar as their regulatory position, as a technology platform, was not clear, concluding it is reasonable to operate while such uncertainty prevailed. Distinct and opposing views to this position were expressed across the regulator community at the time.

Benefit is most likely to have accrued, particularly in the eyes of the public, in favour of the TNC, as seeking to improve for-hire transportation, often in the ace of severe opposition from the incumbent market. The TNC could potentially be seen as an underdog, the new player seeking to offer better and cheaper services in the face of 'big-taxi', a concept leaning on the negatives associated with 'big-alcohol', and 'big-tobacco' of the time. Public support became a part of the lobbying efforts of the new entrants, frequently as an opposition to the taxi industry, and also against the regulators themselves, with city council votes, a political necessity for licensing decisions, now being lobbied by 'big-TNC', rather than 'big-taxi', the former, the TNC, becoming increasingly vocal and receiving increasing public support. Cities that achieved some success in restraining and in some cases banishing the TNCs, most often where their operations were seen as illegal under regulatory law, would face backlashes from the public, now used to and in favour of the new entrant, to the extent that most soon moved to allow TNC entry.

TNCs and Regulations

In previous sections, we have illustrated a somewhat contentious relationship between the TNC and the regulator. In most instances, the regulatory environment has evolved from a historical framework originally designed to avoid specific excesses in the taxi industry. Such controls include limits on numbers intended to reduce destructive competition; controls on vehicle inspection and safety so as to ensure safe vehicles and drivers; and economic controls limiting the presence of monopolistic and similar market abuses. The emergence of the TNC raised distinct questions as to the necessity or even the sense of existing regulations and rightly so in that the app had (the potential) to reduce monopolistic abuses from a lack of competition at the point of use, ironically coupled with the potential to create new (different) monopolies. Further to this, the overall size of the market and distinctly questionable policies for medallion transfer and sale for profit in some locations raised distinct and unanswered questions on the quantity control elements of the traditional regulatory environment.

Not that the market can exist without regulation, or maybe it simply shouldn't, it is the identification of appropriate regulation that forms a key question for the market, its regulators, and suppliers. Amongst the myriad questions this raises, who should regulate, at what level, and with what powers.

The emergence of the TNC in the USA was, at first, most frequently regulated at the city level. The same being true in many, but not all, European locations. City regulatory authorities were already directly engaged in the control of the taxi industry, making them the logical place, for some, for TNC regulation. As a result, many of the existing taxi regulators were given a task to identify how to regulate TNCs, which regulations to apply, and even to decide whether the new entrant was able to operate at all. Many took a view that the TNC in its emerging state should not, or could not, operate under the existing (FHV) regulation, and some made little effort to update regulation to accommodate the newcomer. Much to the TNCs' frustration, multiple efforts on the part of the new entrant to establish and grow faced opposition from the regulatory community presented distinct challenges and a repeated argument seen again and again in city after city. The different scales of operation played a role in the debate, the national and multi-national TNCs facing frequent challenges from the much more localised regulators, with subtle, even minor, differences in the wording and interpretations from authority to authority. The same argument was played out frequently in respect of ostensibly the same legal challenges, creating a pressure to move from the local city level to a minimum state level in the US; provincial level in Canada;[1] and regional and national level in most other countries. Multiple legal challenges followed, including the nature of regulation appropriate, an EU decision of 2017 concluding that TNCs would be regulated as transport companies, rather than technology companies alone.[2]

Other regulatory barriers appear sporadically and are limited to specific locations in some instances. These include but are not limited to: the use and accuracy of the (TNC) app as a metre; the appropriate administrative agency given responsibility for checking driver and vehicle licences; and the appropriate vehicle testing regimes, amongst others.

In the event, an uneasy peace appears to have emerged. Regulatory agencies' responsibilities have settled at a wider geographical scale. In the US, most, but not all, states have assumed regulatory responsibility, while TNC control in European countries has also moved to national and regional scales in most instances. The move from city to regional and national TNC regulation has had, and is likely to continue to have, a negative impact on the traditional taxi industry, remaining at the city level and facing many of the local barriers of which the TNCs complained, restricting and preventing similar scale gains achieved by the new entrant. While new challenges have emerged from unexpected quarters, most recent rights of and responsibilities towards the driving community are discussed below.

Driver Rights

The FHV driver, whether a taxi, private hire, or TNC driver, faces a number of challenges unique to their chosen profession. For the most part, the taxi and TNC drivers are alike in their ability to choose hours, choose to accept work, and even choose to go to work. In the traditional taxi industry, particularly that of the USA, this is expressed as being an independent contractor, often committed to a specific corporate brand, but delivering much at the drivers' own volition, where and when to drive. The corporate brand, say a Yellow, Checker, or Orange taxi company, or indeed any other for that matter, being merely a badge and sometimes a route to dispatch calls in the same way that your favourite coffee chain or fast-food restaurant is quite likely not to be the registered owner of the shop bearing their name.

For the TNC driver, the nature of the service offered differs subtly in that all of the TNC business is directed through the corporate app, though a driver is free to choose which apps, and may, in some locations, be ready to accept calls from two or more apps, though obviously not deliver them simultaneously. The business model created a unique employer/employee relationship dynamic, currently referred to as a 'gig economy'.

The benefit of the situation being the choice to work at will; the downside is that many traditional employee benefits do not apply.

Naming Controversies

The emergence of a new sector has led, perhaps inevitably, to the creation of a range of new questions not common in the existing industry or long since resolved. Obvious amongst these is the appropriate extent of regulation and/or maybe its positioning amongst existing administrative and transport hierarchies. Slightly more surprising is the selection of a category name, alongside, or perhaps as a result of, the many expectations associated with categorisation.

For the straightforward view, the TNC is, with little doubt, a form of on-demand transport operating within the for hire vehicle sector. Slight variations in the overarching mode descriptions may exist, but equally few would dispute the underlying logic that TNCs deliver transport, on-demand, and, generally, for profit. It is notable that all of the same aspects of the FHV categorisation thus far also apply to taxis and private hire. The taxi, as a specific form of FHV, is also noteworthy insofar as its name is long-held and widely understood. Despite the early transfer of naming from hackney carriages to taxis, the name has remained consistent and relates to the service category rather than the company providing that service. Notable, at least for this discussion, the term 'cab' can also be applied to the taxi category, whether as a colloquial English variant, the taxicab, more often used in the USA than elsewhere, or the legal term hackney carriage still maintained in legislation in some places.

The 'mode' term, TNC and its variations, is not so commonly used, with a large number of TNC users making use of a corporate identity, including 'Uber', 'Lyft', 'Ola', 'Grab', 'Bolt', 'Yango' and others. The use as a verb, 'to taxi (home)', being more common than 'to TNC (home)', the latter not being visible to our knowledge in any great extent. The TNC user is more likely 'to Uber (home)', referring to the corporate identity of the app chosen, with anecdotal evidence to support the idea that 'Uber' as a generic term may also encompass other TNC companies. So far, little of controversy, the use of a trade name appears elsewhere across activities and segments, but this reveals only half of the issue and none of its direction.

More pointed perhaps is the historical origins and sensitivities associated with naming conventions. Early iterations of TNC apps in the USA included the term 'Cab', leading to a concern that this may lead to confusion in the eyes of the public that the vehicle was in fact a taxi, a view somewhat confirmed by media references to larger TNC companies as providing taxi dispatching services. Other TNCs concentrating more specifically on the concept of ridesharing, or the provision of lifts, also came under fire for the pre-existing practice of lift-sharing, a category of transport already defined in law in some locations and generally accepted or required to operate without profit.

What emerges is a complex and undecided use of various terms for a series of platforms that cross multiple regulatory boundaries to offer a range of (differing) modal segments a variety of different types of transport. The arrival at a single definition, let alone a single name, is, by default, complicated! Of all aspects, it is the platform that remains the (only) constant across all uses and all (sub)categories. It should be therefore unsurprising that the platform trade name has achieved the prominence that it has and equally highly likely that the platform trade name(s) maintain and expand in their primacy of use. Legal terms applied in larger locations, including the use of transportation network company in North America is likely to remain critical in much the same way that hackney carriage remains a legal term for taxis in some locations. Furthermore, the integration of taxis into the larger platform offerings may yet further cement the concept that the TNC is indeed a taxi: this time without the critique or opposition of the traditional taxi trade who, by dint of their inclusion, are exactly that, part of the TNC offering.

Notes

1 Not all Canadian provinces exert regulatory authority on TNCs, with a number, including Saskatchewan, at the time of writing, remaining under the jurisdiction of the cities within the province.
2 The legal decision of the European Court of Justice in 2017 concluded that Uber was subject to regulation as a transportation company (see Hacker, 2018).

References

Bonini, S., and Capizzi, V., (2019) 'The role of venture capital in the emerging entrepreneurial finance ecosystem: Future threats and opportunities', *Venture Capital*, 21(2–3), pp. 137–175, doi:10.1080/13691066.2019.1608697

Hacker, P., (2018) 'UberPop, UberBlack, and the regulation of digital platforms after the Asociación Profesional elite taxi judgment of the CJEU', *European Review of Contract Law*, 14(1), pp. 80–96. doi:10.1515/ERCL-2018-1005

Horan, H., (2017) 'Will the growth of Uber increase economic welfare', *Transport Law Journal*, 44, p. 33.

Lerner, J., and Nanda, R., (2020) 'Venture capital's role in financing innovation: What we know and how much we still need to learn', *Journal of Economic Perspectives*, 34(3), pp. 237–261. doi:10.1257/jep.34.3.237

Matherne, B.P. and O'Toole, J., (2017) 'Uber: aggressive management for growth', *The CASE Journal*, 13(4), pp. 561–586. doi:10.1108/TCJ-10-2015-0062

Sarwar, M. and Soomro, T.R., (2013) 'Impact of smartphones on society', *European Journal of Scientific Research*, 98(2), pp. 216–226. ISSN 1450-216X/1450-202X

10 Future Planning, Regulation, and Rebirth

The taxi, it was argued by Gilbert and Samuels (1982), was an *'urban survivor'*. The same is true, in our review, of all for hire vehicles (FHVs), including transportation network companies (TNCs). It being that demand for the mode exists and is likely to continue, or, if you prefer, for the style of transport, being available at short notice for engagement with driver for individual transport and/or the transport of small groups. Measurable demand is apparent for transport on demand, across all of the existing methods of engagement in practically all city locations and a large swathe of peri-urban and rural communities. The extent of demand suggests FHVs are likely to remain part of the urban mobility landscape into the foreseeable future.

The FHV market is, by its nature and repeated provision, intuitive and common in most locations, though not static, as demonstrated by the success of apps and their impact on the traditional market. As in previous points of change, including motorisation, as well as the earlier integration of radios and dispatch systems, as technologies have evolved, so has the FHV market. The inclusion of change is an inherent part of the market itself. Inherent to the market is also its relationship with its regulators and the regulatory framework surrounding it. To further complicate the analysis, the links between the market and the regulator, the political framework in which regulations are defined, and the relative scales of provision across differing operator 'types'.

The past decade has seen significant change within the industry, with many of the economic constraints and issues affecting the taxi being impacted by the emerging technologies. These include issues arising from information asymmetries, between driver and customer, addressed using smartphones with access to third-party verification. The decade has also seen advances in consumer interfaces and dispatch, while some pricing-, competition-, and labour-related issues have yet to be addressed.

In this chapter, we will present a cross-section of elements likely to influence the future of the FHV industry. We will review re-occurring market issues likely to remain and review the nature of regulatory responses to these. The chapter concludes by drawing together common outcomes and suggesting future direction of the industry, its regulators, and users.

DOI: 10.4324/9781003256311-11

Future Planning

In the previous chapters of this book, we have charted the development of the current FHV market to date. Against this history and current baseline, we look forward to speculating on developments likely to occur in a future characterised by complexity, dilemma, and counter-trends. We consider the impacts across a diverse set of actors and interests involved at the local, national, and global level, concluding on the developments that can be suggested as more likely, and review the contexts of that change.

Broad Societal Trends That Influence Mobility

Myriad views exist of the future trends in transport, as in many other activities. Enoch (2015) argues of a future convergence of mode choice towards automated shared taxis encompassing a current trend in autonomous vehicle design, and a change in vehicle ownership models, partly as a result of their relatively high, sunk, initial cost. Others, including Aarhaug and Olsen (2018), develop scenarios based on expert interviews and survey data that argue on the basis of a trajectory for specific modes. Both strands incorporate elements of behaviour and economic context, in transition studies defined as the socio-techical 'landscape', broadly the context surrounding the market, and the influence of resulting contexts on changing mobility behaviours. Elements of these are described below.

Economic Growth

In most cases, a strong link exists between increased income and increased consumption, a basic economic tenet that can be applied to the majority of goods and services, including travel. In short, richer people travel more and are more inclined to use private and energy-intensive means of transport, though some exceptions to this exist, while greater disposable income can also lead to increased demand for economic activities, including those increasing demand for travel. In the mode choice context, this will often correlate to an increased use of private car, taxis, and aircraft, use (of all) of which tend to increase with income.

Key exceptions to this can relate to environmental awareness, which can relate to relative cost of a more friendly environmental choice (effectively a Giffen Good), or where a significant investment in public transport creates a transit benefit/shift in user behaviour choice.

The effect of economic growth, where resulting in increased individual incomes, is likely to be positive on the demand for FHVs.

Demographic Changes

The link between transport and population is also positive and illustrated by an increased level of urbanisation as global populations grow. Ageing populations are also felt to be more likely to urbanise.

All of these trends point in the direction of increased demand for FHVs. In addition, sub-components such as better health suggest that people will remain mobile later in life. Generation effects suggest increased mobility, as 40-year-old people now travel more than people the same age travelled 20 years ago. This is likely to influence FHV demand, but unknown in which direction, as the demand for traditional taxis had been falling before the arrival of TNCs but has reversed significantly since their launch.

Behavioural Changes

Technological developments have, in general, resulted in an increasing opportunity space and will therefore have an effect not dissimilar to that of economic growth. Noted that both technological, demographic, and climate effects are likely to be simplifications – not everyone will benefit from advances in mobility technology, while climate change mitigation points in the opposite direction, distinct behavioural patterns are visible.

Large unknowns should also be acknowledged with respect to the future availability and direction of technologies. In 2017, few would guess that shared e-scooters would become a major mobility option in many cities; but these had, by 2021, achieved more trips in Oslo than taxis and TNCs combined (Ruter, 2021). The future of autonomous vehicles needs to also be questioned, perhaps in terms of timescale – the when more than the if. Studies also suggest that autonomous vehicles will be more likely in the FHV market in their early development and influence this market, in addition to transforming the market for private cars.

Developments Directly Affecting the FHV Market

In the previous section, we suggested that a link existed between increasing income and the use of private transport options. The uptake of private options, as opposed to public transport, can also reflect the development of technology and the relative position of FHV transport between private and public modes. In short, the costs associated with using private mobility options, including TNCs, has seen a decrease as a function of developments in technology, outpacing the potential benefits of similar technologies on public shared modes. This suggests the conclusion that digitalisation reduces transaction and coordination costs; although neither is likely to directly influence the cost of operating a vehicle, both influence other associated costs: direct costs, such as dispatching, taximeters, and payment; and indirect costs such as verification and information on vehicle/trip. In addition, the move towards electric vehicles may further reduce the marginal cost of vehicle operations. All of these factors point towards a decreased cost of production, the cost of delivering a FHV trip; and, by extension, an increased use of FHV. Opposing factors are also significant and may include: the development of micro-mobility, which has a negative impact on taxi use in particular at night (Fearnley, 2022) and for shorter trips.

When systematising the likely influence of future developments on the FHV markets, some general findings emerge. Street and rank taxi hailing are likely to continue a measured loss in market share/relative importance to the travelling public, and by extension to the industry itself.

As booking through intermediaries becomes easier and more efficient, the use of 'new systems' will increase. From the passenger's perspective, the need to hail will reduce, with a potential/perceived reduction in any risk associated with street hailing. The adoption of app bookings, whether to TNCs or conventional actors, is highly likely to continue to increase, not only as part of an overall increase in traffic volumes expected for the FHV industry but also as a result of people actively preferring to book via an app intermediary rather than direct interaction with the driver. Such developments will continue to result in a shift in regulation, possibly reducing the need to maintain the same patterns of regulation previously applied. Significant factors include:

1   The apparent reduction in the (regulatory) need to address information asymmetry between passenger and driver, as the interaction becomes more and more likely to be handled through an intermediary. Potentially offset by the continued availability of hailing a taxi as an option.
2   Competition between intermediaries (TNCs or dispatchers) is likely to become more important. The issue here being the emergence of anti-competitive behaviour, including the development of local monopolies, where the intermediary can act as a dominant actor both in selling services to the public and in purchasing services from the vehicle owners and drivers.
3   Labour issues are likely to remain important, particularly where the shift towards booking through intermediaries does not change the underlying structure of the industry. If anything, the challenges for labour safety are likely to get more difficult as the value chain becomes longer.
4   Intermodal competition may become a more important point for regulation. This is a result of FHV gaining market shares. Private FHV uses more space and energy than public transport (mass transit) and is therefore more likely to increase congestion and environmental footprint of urban mobility, in parallel with increased utility for the consumers. This may well result in an increased need for local policies for addressing mode split issues as the best solutions for the city may be different than the solution that arises from the sum of individual choices.

Developments Lead by the Taxi Industry

It is easy to portray the taxi industry as a set of passive actors responding to developments in the outside world, rather than informing them. For a large part, this is not the case. The active role of the sector has become clearer with the development of technologies. Allowing the bundling of services to become increasingly prominent.

The development follows two main directions:

1   Where FHV companies branch out to other mobility or logistics markets, including delivery, micro-mobility, shared vehicles, and scheduled services; examples include Grab, Uber, and Bolt. This can be seen as a 'natural path' for tech-centred companies but is a wider phenomenon.
2   Where companies not directly involved in transport or logistics provision bundle FHV services with other mobility options, with examples including Yandex and MaaS Global.

Recurring Market Issues and Regulation

Multiple studies highlight the tendency of the FHV market to become dominated by small actors (Cooper et al., 2016). The phenomenon is not unique to the vehicle for hire sector alone and can be seen across logistics providers, where small independent companies typically operate the vehicles and coordination (dispatching) is handled separately. The development is focused on the capital requirements for operation, as relatively limited, with economies of scale in coordination possible separately from the operation of the vehicles. Both Pagano and McKnight (1983) and Arnott (1996) conclude that there is a case for economies of scale in vehicle coordination, with examples well documented both theoretically and empirically. Little documentation exists, in contrast, in respect of the economies of scale from vehicle operation.

Underlying economic properties may be the reason for the observed tendency of a segmentation along the value chain. Where coordinating actors increase in scale, the operating actors remain small and independent economic units. The pattern was present in the taxi market before the arrival of TNCs but has increased in relevance with the arrival of TNCs. This tendency also has parallels across the gig economy or platform economy in other sectors. This is a form of specialisation. However, it is also a form of fragmentation of responsibilities.

The latter component has labour implications which have resulted in a number of studies. A common development is that full-time professional actors are complemented by or replaced by part-time semi-professionals or part-time workers. This development includes a movement towards increasing inequalities in terms of power, to the detriment of established workers. Felstiner (2011) argues that this is a form of 'crowdsourcing' where tasks that would traditionally be addressed by an employee are distributed to a large pool of potential workers available on call. Efficiency is to some extent replaced by redundancy. However, although often associated with the introduction of TNCs, this form of work has a long history in the FHV sector. The difference is more in terms of scale than content (Leiren and Aarhaug, 2016). In either case, basing supply on a large pool of part-time workers is dependent on the availability of that labour pool.

Market Issues at the Vehicle Level

A recurring issue at the vehicle level relates to the relationships between the driver, the customer, coordinator, and public authorities. This is unlikely to change with technology, although the problem will most likely get smaller over time with more and more customers opting out of street hail.

For the customer, there is a need to verify that the driver is safe and reliable. This is difficult as the market is likely to be atomistic, where both parties can credibly assume that they will not meet again after the single interaction. The customer is placing her/him-self in an exposed position, in particular if travelling alone, for personal safety and the avoidance of price abuse. The same risks existing in the reverse, where the driver needs to know that the customer is not going to stack them, vandalise the vehicle, or avoid payment. Such mutual insecurities can be, and to a large extent are, solved by including a third party in the transaction – whether the TNC, the dispatcher, or the regulatory authority. TNCs in general do this well, by requiring both driver and passenger to be identifiable, while traditional methods of addressing risk through the regulators may be less immediate. Traditional approaches have included regulatory scrutiny of driver backgrounds and driving record, while requiring use of taximeters to ensure appropriate fare charging and vehicle markings in respect of reporting and follow up, the evaluation of the passenger falling to the driver/dispatcher, at the point of use, and in some instances, leading to trip denials, often on spurious or prejudicial grounds.

The relationship between the driver and the coordinator/dispatcher, vehicle owner, or a platform is ongoing and likely to reflect industry particularities that may differ from other forms of work. The industry differs from some in the measurements of effort and result. A lack of such measurement leads to an industry-specific assessment of effort and remuneration. Various payment schemes can exist; the most common typically allocates income risk, and sometimes cost risk, to the driver, either by requiring the driver to pay a leasing fee for hiring the vehicle for the duration of the shift, allowing the driver to keep all earnings; or by income sharing, where the revenue is split between the driver and the vehicle owner. Both these schemes can result in large fluctuations in daily income to the driver, and both are present both in traditional taxi operation and TNC operation. The flip side of risk allocation is that the driver is exposed to an income risk, which is likely to affect and influence those who chose to work in the industry.

The relationship between the driver and regulator is also highly dependent on the form that taxi regulations take and how these are put into practice. In areas where licensing is used to address wider issues, such as wages and quality, that relationship is likely to be complex. In other areas, where the regulation is devolved to private companies, such as dispatchers or TNCs, the risk moves from the authority to the operator, changing the nature of control required at a government level, where the regulator is more likely to adopt a role in definition and verification of standards rather than individual behaviour.

City Level Issues

At the city level, regulatory issues can also include the image of the city itself, external and internal to the city, suggesting policies that may promote a clean or attractive FHV service, and possibly the common appearance or uniform colours seen in some cities, including Washington DC, by design, and London UK, by default. In practice, significant variations to this approach exist, but most cities will conclude that having an FHV sector that is perceived as poor by visitors would create a problem for that city. This is likely to remain an issue in the future. Critical issues identified at the city level include the fair treatment of passengers, pricing levels, congestion at stands or in the street, the physical appearance of the fleet, etc. These are often perceived as being something the city or city region would like to influence as these are often perceived as local issues.

Regulations to ensure the fair treatment of passengers, in particular the disabled, can be difficult to enforce. Disabled passengers can be associated with extra costs, most frequently the time of loading and additional assistance required, though this will most often ignore the additional income generation of an additional trip. Historically, this has resulted in a lower number of services provided for people with disabilities, often in direct contravention of equality legislation, and sometimes, reflecting real prejudice amongst drivers, at the same time, as the general population receives better service. Other arguments in this respect include the need for special or dedicated vehicles with features such as wheelchair accessibility, argued as more expensive to purchase and created a series of court cases seeking to reduce discrimination. In purely economic terms, the argument can be made that the market outcome, without regulation, would be a lower level of service at a higher price to disabled passengers, a fundamental plank of accessibility regulation and a good illustration of market failure for specific market segments. Despite a cross-section of anti-discrimination legislation, the occurrence of discriminatory practices and illegal trip refusals continues to this day.

In terms of pricing, the analysis as to what extent prices are fair requires systematic statistics on transactions or direct regulatory intervention such as through an enforced maximum fare. This is more of an issue where street hail is a dominant form of vehicle engagement, as compared to a situation where passengers can get credible information on prices before a decision is being made. However, charging different fares to different segments of the population or in different parts of the city may be perceived as being unfair. And possibly discriminatory. The need to monitor the prices increases with the complexity of the fare structure.

Street congestion is an issue faced at the city level and is associated with a move from production efficiency to redundancy often associated with crowd working (Leiren and Aarhaug, 2016; Aarhaug and Olsen, 2018). In other words, in a situation where the transport intermediary is not under significant direct pressure from the transport operators, it is better for the intermediary to focus on having more vehicles on the street than to attempt to optimise the use of the existing vehicles. The negative externality is mainly faced by the city, in the form of increased congestion, and to a lesser extent by the drivers/vehicle owners in the form of lower efficiency. A number of cities in Europe, and some Asian markets, have sought a specific split between modes for trips within their region. This can often include limits applied to the polluting modes, such as private cars and taxis. Examples in the UK include the development of low emissions zones, while other countries, such as France, require the display of emissions permits on vehicles creating a graduated system of control and limitation. Other examples include area-based supplementary charging, sometimes called congestion charging, highlighting both the range of and need for effective tools that can influence modal split. These, in turn, require detailed statistics on vehicle utilisation and the possibility to enforce various forms of congestion or environmental impact taxation.

There are also instances where the cities are purchasers of transport services where the role of the city as a regulator and purchaser may come into conflict. However, irrespective of this potential conflict of interest at the city level, it is in the public's interest that there exists a functioning market for the purchase of these services from private operators. This means that a minimum of competition and availability of suitable vehicles in the area must be ensured.

Global Issues

A review of the trends affecting mobility and mobility policy suggests the possibility of convergence globally, where global cities become increasingly similar in terms of demographics. These may include small segments of the urban population with high income levels and larger segments working in service industries, including traditional taxi driving, and an increased reliance on gig economy jobs, including TNCs.

Global cities in this definition would face the same or similar issues with respect to the FHV market, particularly where global players sought standardisation across regulations. To date, most regulation occurs at a local level, the major difference arising from globalisation shifts in the relative power between authorities at the city level and TNCs operating at the global level, with a demonstrable shift towards standardisation in the favour of TNCs.

Theoretical Issues That May Become More Prominent

In earlier sections, we underlined a range of theoretical issues associated with the FHV markets. Many issues reflect the long history of the mode, with a number continuing despite the range of technologies that evolved and emerged over their lifetime. Some of these, including those that stem from information asymmetries, could, potentially, be largely solved by the technological developments they have witnessed, while others are likely to remain or even become more important. In this section, we consider the areas of theory that have emerged and appear prominent.

Utility Maximisation

A problem in network economics relates to the utility derived from a marginal increase in service level may display greater benefit to its users than to its producers. This can result in the situation where an open market is likely to undersupply, pointing towards a social optimum that would only be attained through subsidisation of the service. Arnott (1996) argues that this is the case for taxi services. His argument being that there are public benefit gains of a subsidised taxi service, through network effects. The market, however, is based on a long tradition of operations without direct support, in direct contrast to other forms of public transport modes, that typically receive extensive subsidies in developed countries. The suggestion is that theoretical arguments for subsidising might be just as valid for FHV nodes as for scheduled public transport.

The flip side of the network economics argument for subsidising FHV is the observation that personal vehicles are under-priced (Wangsness et al., 2020). The argument is also valid for FHVs, and in particular, in situations where a significant proportion of driven kilometres are driven without passengers on congested roads. The subsidy of FHVs would effectively further distort the overall transport market. The issue is common across many cities and may be considered an underlying intermodal problem where users do not pay the full cost of the disutility their use inflicts on others in the form of congestion and local emissions. The under-pricing argument may well outweigh the internal utility maximisation problem of the FHV industry and remains a consistent and unsolved problem in most western societies.

Economies of Scale TNCs and Digital Platforms

A discussion that remains unresolved and related to TNCs is whether or not it is a case where the winner will take all. In other words, that the economies of scale in vehicle coordination through digital platforms point towards a market dominated by one or a few global actors. We will argue that this is not an obvious outcome. The reasoning behind this is decreasing utility of an extra unit of information and low costs of switching between TNCs for both passengers and drivers.

Goldfarb and Tucker (2019) argue that digitalisation, of the dispatch service in the FHV industry, reduces replication costs and transaction costs. Related to this is the argument that the quality of a digital service is at least in part dependent on the use of AI methods: a function of the volume of data available for analysis, which, in turn, is likely to be a function of the number of actors connected to the platform. However, as in all statistics, although there is always a positive utility of adding an observation to a dataset, the utility of each additional unit decreases with the number of units in the dataset. Thus, the added utility of one vehicle or passenger more is much larger if the platform is organising 1,000 as opposed to if it is organising 1,000,000 users. This means that although there are large economies of scale associated with the TNC, these are likely to decrease as the size of the platform increases. This has the effect that it is cheaper to catch up than to develop the market. It is acknowledged that initial design and setup has high initial costs but not as high as the cost endured by the first actor. Technical solutions can be mimicked, and although costly, a user base can be "purchased". This again means that it will be difficult to achieve long-run profitability for a TNC if it is not actively changing the content of its service or protected from competition.

The observation of market entry and marginal utility has parallels in the 'empty core problem' (Sjostrom, 1993; Button, 1996), where long-term profitability is hard to achieve without market intervention. This may help explain part of the extensive action to create a form of regulatory capture. In this case, to limit market entry at a key level in the value chain, either through legal protection or anticompetitive behaviour. This line of action has traditionally been at the vehicle level by the established vehicle or medallion owners. But is now more often argued for at the dispatcher or TNC level. In extension, this argument highlights a key challenge for regulatory authorities and political entities as to how they prevent market capture.

Regulatory Solutions

Both the re-occurring market issues and the theoretical issues that may become more pressing in the future have a series of possible known solutions.

Issues with a Dominant Actor

Although the market outcomes, and market equilibria, of the current TNC-dominated FHV industry remain to be seen, some lessons from history suggest a goal for future regulation. Previous sections have suggested it to be unclear whether or not the possibility exists to achieve a stable market with a dominant TNC as market leader. Whether this can be achieved through market forces, or regulation, given the possibility of capture or other forms of anticompetitive behaviour.

It is equally clear from empirical studies that several TNCs believe that an outcome with one market dominating actor capturing super-profits is an achievable future scenario. This belief can be illustrated by the fact many TNCs are willing to operate with large losses in order to establish a dominant position in the market and extract rent from that position in the future.

The outcome of a dominant actor exerting excessive and unregulated control is likely not in the public's interest, however. Though the willingness of an authority to act to reduce abuse, or the public's willingness to accept such regulations may be limited by the effectiveness of messaging and presentation. Several policy measures do in fact exist and can be introduced in order to avoid the most egregious negative outcomes. These include multi-homing, market monitoring, and auctioning.

Multi-homing

One measure to support a competitive market on the coordination level is to prevent TNCs from claiming exclusivity from the drivers. In other words, the drivers should be allowed to connect to more than one TNC at any given point in time. This would contribute to a competitive market between TNCs. If a TNC tries to take a cut which is substantially higher than the competition, both driver and passenger can easily just change platform.

A downside to this regulation is that it removes the TNCs possibility to monitor the vehicle. The TNC cannot check if the driver works 15 hour + shifts and is a safety risk due to fatigue. To counter this, some authority, separate from the TNCs, must independently monitor the market. This can include vehicle monitoring acting independently of the TNCs, amongst others.

Market Monitoring

In many cities, market dominance can be hard to determine. As long as prices and service levels appear at a reasonable level, it is possible to assume that the market is functioning correctly, even in instances where one dominant actor is present. The threat of market entry from a competitor may be enough to discipline the incumbent, described as a contestable market (Baumol, 1982). However, in order to be certain of this, prices and activity levels need to be constantly monitored. This means that the regulating authority must have sufficient means and power to conduct monitoring of variables such as prices, trips, vehicles, and drivers and to issue fines or other measures for enforcing compliance with the necessary reporting scheme.

Auctioning

An argument may also exist for service auctioning (franchising). The concept arises where a natural monopoly exists, in the FHV industry, in relation to service coordination. The action of auctioning, franchising, or tendering provides a solution that has been seen in European public transport markets, particularly in the case of mobility services. Examples of franchised or tendered can range from rail, local public transport, to shared bikes and e-scooters and in some cases integrated ticketing and travel planning, giving rise to comparison with the FHV dispatch service.

Such systems allow for a limited number of actors to be selected by the city on the basis of a public tender and given market protection, albeit temporary in some instances. Tenders and auctions can include fees which vary between direct payment and assurances of service provision. In most cases, the approach requires a city to define and provide high levels of service standard requirements (specifications) that can, and will be, carefully monitored. This model has gained interest and is increasingly applied to public transport provision (Wong et al., 2020).

These possible regulatory interventions represent possibilities to prevent private monopolies from being established at the local (city) level. However, they all rest on the requirement that local authorities need to both have a legal framework, allowing these regulations and the practical capacity to enforce compliance.

Ensuring Safe Vehicles

The requirement, of an authority, to ensure that both driver and vehicle are safe appears relatively self-evident. The issue, however, has been argued over decades and centuries and likely to remain critical to regulation irrespective of technological development.

Safety can be addressed by a combination of regulatory authority, including standardised driving tests and vehicle inspections, and/or in-house controls applied by the operator, the latter model gaining traction amongst TNCs. In the latter case, a typical approach is to deploy feedback loops using mutual ratings of issues that can be assessed on the basis of qualitative review. However, the TNC internal regulation is unlikely to be sufficient to more major technical issues, nor effective in fleets where a passenger can avoid the automated processes of engagement, e.g. continue to hail or engage at stand. The range of levels of control, and the possible avoidance of these for some trips, continues to suggest the need for minimum standards checks and inspections to be maintained at an authority level (Aarhaug and Skollerud, 2014).

Congestion and Modal Split

Linked to the theoretical issues of utility maximisation in a situation with economies of density relates to the practical problems in deciding service levels.

At the city level, the issue relates to the need to create and maintain a reasonable level of service and cost, for both the public and operators. The extensive externalities produced by a large number of private car-sized vehicles in a city with limited space means that economic arguments exist for limiting the role of FHV vehicles. On one hand, the FHV may function as a complement to a non-private vehicle lifestyle, empirical studies have shown that TNCs can in fact draw ridership away from other less polluting modes and create an induced demand (Rayle et al., 2016), which is good in terms of maximising utility at the individual level but may run in conflict with overall policies to reduce the environmental impact of mobility.

There are several possible regulatory measures to address these issues. These include congestion pricing, road pricing, and charging a fee for empty driving or cruising between fares. These regulations can be applied both to private and commercial vehicles but require monitoring and enforcing. The measures are also likely to be unpopular and would, as a result, need to be carefully constructed in order to address the issues at hand without having undue distributional effects. For many cities, the options available remain underused, the example of congestion pricing being adopted by only a small number of locations, with similar outcomes for workplace charging levies, at least at the time of writing. Statements of climate emergencies may also fall on deaf, or at least hearing impaired, ears, as an ambiguous concept. At the same time, defined measures, such as the reduction of 20% in vehicle kms in Scotland, is likely to have unduly or disproportionately more severe impacts on rural communities and those with limited incomes.

A different approach could be to introduce a minimum fare or capping supply. Both can be done by applying 'smart regulation' as opposed to the traditional caps and fare regulations that were introduced in the 1930s. Both will also require monitoring and enforcing in order to work.

Labour

The freedom and flexibility to work at will, common to most of the taxi trade, is both an advantage and a disadvantage for the FHV industry labour market. On one hand, the freedom allows the individual the possibility to work when convenient, whether to earn a bit extra on top of alternative work, or simply to define a work–life balance not available in more traditional working patterns, but it also places the income risk at the operator or driver level, with very limited possibilities for influencing working conditions. This challenge persists with the TNCs.

Drivers are often recruited from groups with limited choices on the labour market, and these are often dependent on the vehicle owners or platforms (Cutolo and Kenney, 2019; Oppegaard, 2021).

Disabilities

Transport provision for passengers with disabilities also provides a focus and a series of conflicts for the FHV industry. Many of the arguments appear focused on the specific issues related to the carriage of passengers with wheelchairs, but this should not be considered necessarily the only form of disability deserving attention, nor indeed the main issue. For the intending user, the issue is related to equality of access and effectively fair treatment alongside all other passengers, with a large number of regulations and more generic legislation acting to support such rights. In the US, this is exempted by the Americans with Disabilities Act (ADA), in the UK the Equalities Act, and a wide range of similar laws worldwide.

For the FHV supplier, the issue is often stylised as one of cost. The accessible vehicle, often meaning the wheelchair accessible vehicle (WAV), can be more expensive than a standard saloon (sedan), and this has had the effect of a lower level of access across the taxi industry than would represent equal treatment. Persons with disabilities typically also travel less and have less interaction with broader society (Gregersen and Flotve, 2021), though the extent that this is associated with an absence of the appropriate vehicle types is argued, often in court.

In addition to being more dependent on accessible taxi services, disabled passengers can be put at a further disadvantage where FHV services are deregulated, mainly as a result of requirements for wheelchair accessible vehicles and other special needs accommodation being costly to supply. In a market where operators can cut costs by not providing disability-friendly services, either through vehicles or engagement methods, this is done as illustrated by the liberalisation in Norway (Aarhaug et al., 2020). Operator incentives leave the most reliant of the FHVs, with lower levels of service, while the majority of the population enjoys higher levels of availability.

There are many ways that this effect can be mitigated, either at the vehicle or fleet level, but this typically requires either regulatory intervention in the form of requirement or subsidies or legal entitlements.

References

Aarhaug, J. and Olsen, S., (2018) 'Implications of ride-sourcing and self-driving vehicles on the need for regulation in unscheduled passenger transport', *Research in Transportation Economics*, 69, pp. 573–582. doi:10.1016/j.retrec.2018.07.026.

Aarhaug, J., Oppegaard, S.M.N., Gundersen, F., Hartveit, K.J.L., Skollerud, K. and Dapi, B., (2020) *Drosjer i Norge fram mot 2020*, TØI-rapport, 1802/2020, Oslo: Transportøknomisk institutt.

Aarhaug, J. and Skollerud, K., (2014) 'Taxi: Different solutions in different segments', *Transportation Research Procedia*, 1, pp. 276–283.

Arnott, R., (1996) 'Taxi travel should be subsidized', *Journal of Urban Economics*, 40(3), pp. 316–333. doi:10.1006/juec.1996.0035

Baumol, W., Panzar, J. and Willig, R., (1983) 'Contestable markets: An uprising in the theory of industry structure: Reply', *American Economic Review*, 73, pp. 491–496.

Button, K., (1996) 'Liberalising European aviation: Is there an empty core problem?', *Journal of Transport Economics and Policy*, 30, pp. 275–291.

Cooper, J., Mundy, R. and Nelson, J., (2016) *Taxi! Urban economies and the social and transport impacts of the taxicab*. London: Routledge.

Cutolo, D. and Kenney, M., (2019) *Platform-dependent entrepreneurs: Power asymmetries, risks, and strategies in the platform economy*. Available at SSRN: https:// ssrn.com/ abstract=3372560, doi:10.2139/ssrn.3372560

Dotterud Leiren, M. and Aarhaug, J., (2016) Taxis and crowd-taxis: Sharing as a private activity and public concern. *Internet Policy Review*, [online] 5(2). Available at: https://policyreview.info/articles/analysis/taxis-and-crowd-taxis-sharing-private-activity-and-public-concern [Accessed: 1 August 2022].

Enoch, M.P., (2015) 'How a rapid modal convergence into a universal automated taxi service could be the future for local passenger transport', *Technology Analysis & Strategic Management*, 27, pp. 910–924. doi:10.1080/09537325.2015.1024646

Fearnley, N., (2022) 'Factors affecting e-scooter mode substitution', *Findings*, June. doi:10.32866/001c.36514

Felstiner, A., (2011) *Working the crowd: Employment and labor law in the crowdsourcing industry*, 32, p. 143.

Gilbert, G. and Samuels, R.E., (1982) *The taxicab: An urban transportation survivor.* Chapel Hill: University of North Carolina Press.

Goldfarb, A. and Tucker, C., (2019) 'Digital economics', *Journal of Economic Literature*, 57, pp. 3–43.

Gregersen, F.A. and Flotve, B.L., (2021) 'Funksjonsnedsettelser', *dybdeanalyse av den nasjonale reisevaneundersøkelsen* 2018/19, TØI-rapport, Oslo: Transportøkonomisk institutt.

Oppegaard, S.M.N. (2021) 'Regulating flexibility: Uber's platform as a technological work arrangement', *Nordic Journal of Working Life Studies*, 11(1) pp. 109–127. https://doi.org/10.18291/njwls.122197.

Pagano, A. M. and McKnight, C.E., (1983) 'Economies of scale in the taxicab industry: Some empirical evidence from the United States', *Journal of Transport Economics and Policy*, 17(3), pp. 299–313.

Rayle, L., Dai, D., Chan, N., Cervero, R. and Shaheen, S., (2016) 'Just a better taxi? A survey-based comparison of taxis, transit, and ridesourcing services in San Francisco', *Transport Policy*, 45, pp. 168–178.

Ruter, (2021) *Market information survey (MIS) 2017-2021*. In: RUTER (ed.). available on request.

Sjostrom, W., (1993) 'Antitrust immunity for shipping conferences: An empty core approach', *Antitrust Bulletin*.

Wangsness, P.B., Proost, S. and Rødseth, K.L. (2020) 'Vehicle choices and urban transport externalities. Are Norwegian policy makers getting it right', *Transportation Research Part D. Transport and Environment*, ISSN 1361–9209, doi:10.1016/j.trd.2020.102384

Wong, Y.Z., Hensher, D. and Mulley, C., (2020) 'Mobility as a service (MaaS): Charting a future context', *Transportation Research Part A: Policy and Practice*, 131, pp. 5–19, ISSN 0965-8564, doi:10.1016/j.tra.2019.09.030

11 Review and Conclusions, the Taxi as an Intuitive and Recurring Mode

Taxis and for hire vehicles (FHVs) have a history that dates back to decades and centuries. The concept of a taxi, rather than the vehicle itself, predates most other forms of transport and would likely have formed the earliest recognisable form of passenger carriage with driver for a fee. The distinction of requiring a driver, and a fee (fare), separates the vehicle from self-driven transport which would, presumably, have paralleled the first FHVs. The development of Taxi Regulations first appear rapidly after the introduction of the vehicle itself, usually seeking to address, or at least respond to, an element of operation that created friction, appeared hazardous, or worked against the public interest.

Early regulations, as with later reforms, could also reflect lobby interests, including those ascribed to the London Boatman in response to and opposing the launch of the mode. Many variations of the same theme have been documented ever since.

Today, the FHV mode appears commonplace, even universal amongst urban populations. A majority of taxi operations characteristics have become standardised in many, but not all, respects. The service appears so intuitive that its operation is known without further description worldwide. The act of 'taxiing' is broadly the same regardless of city, country, or user. The relative consistency and broad understanding of the mode belies the fact that underneath the veneer of a single product, many subtle and legislated differences can exist. The mode is and has remained subject to significant amounts of regulation, being subject to regulations that appear to have changed little despite the plethora of changes experienced by the mode itself.

The current mode bears little physical resemblance to its ancestors. Vehicles have become motorised, both electrified, moving to internal combustion engine vehicles, and back to electrification over the course of about a century. The industry is adapting to and adopting the technologies of the time, as being the case in a vast majority of similar trades. The current market upheaval reflects both the fashion and technological advances of the smartphone, even though the significant benefits of the emerging technologies appear to face struggles and difficulties. Notable is not just the opposition of the trade, having invested in a previous set of technologies, but the method

DOI: 10.4324/9781003256311-12

by which the regulatory community appears to have misunderstood, misjudged, and even contributed to losses within an industry otherwise likely to benefit. Core to this is the misunderstandings of the regulatory community, the de facto creation of market contradictions comprising incompatible forms of market delivery, each openly hostile to the other. Fundamental misunderstandings of market form are also common, while the apparent conflict between a competitive market operating under regulated competition and its, incompatible, alternative of open market competition appears only infrequently in analyses.

The current market upheaval, having been made possible by the emergence of smartphone applications and platform organisation, is only the latest in a line of significant market changes but possibly also the largest and most straining so far. The most significant effects of the current technological revolution in the industry appear linked to organisation and control; while previous events included both vehicle and dispatch technologies, the current tranche are concentrated on not only improvements in digital technologies, contributing to better economics of scale in fleet coordination, but also on the operational and control freedoms granted, often unwittingly, to the new market entrant and denied from the existing, incumbent, trade.

New app technologies have not only allowed for a streamlining of the passenger and driver experiences but also, probably more importantly, allowed for different organisational structures to emerge. The location services aspects of the app, live mapping, and instant location definitions can also shift the skills required of the driver, reducing reliance on pre-existing 'local' knowledge, from the list of driver qualifications, and eliminate the need for the dispatcher to have any specific local area knowledge. The changes in perquisite qualifications are changing the industry.

App development has increased the role of FHVs as a part of the local transport system as well, increasing the use of the FHV sector as a whole, while typically leading to steep declines in the use of traditional taxis and traditional private hire vehicles (PHVs). While the sector can demonstrate a positive outcome, by drawing rides away from private cars, a negative is also observed by drawing passengers away from public transport. The benefits of reduced private car use need to be balanced against a declining bus and transit use, oftentimes, placing pressures on the economics of the traditional bus service sector. Furthermore, as a number of locations had traditionally drawn on cross-subsidy within the taxi mode to support accessibility and human services transport, the declining taxi base incomes would be likely to have a negative impact on socially required/desirable services. While transportation network companies (TNCs) have made, high-profile, efforts to accommodate and supply socially beneficial services, the practice is limited and not particularly widespread. TNC efforts to support cities such as Boston, as an example of good practice, can be immediately lost to cities where such services have been denied, such as New Orleans. The suggestion is possible that TNCs' interest is related purely to immediate profitability.

Review of the Current Market

Today's taxi market has come a long way from its historical origins. The market is typified by a mix of actors, cultures, and institutions that have emerged and evolved over centuries, alongside controls and regulations developed over much the same period. Some of the elements that are present have probably remained past their expiry date, while others may still be highly relevant. As the market continues to operate in many of the same ways as the markets of the 18th century, so too the needs to avoid exploitative, abusive, and/or monopolistic behaviours remain. Critical to the justification of market control is the validity of its need and its design. The ultimate validity of the need is linked to protecting the public. To remain justified regulation need to be designed so that they can be applied fairly across all market participants, and be effective, the latter require enforceability. As a result, market controls must result in the market avoiding the negatives the regulation was designed to mitigate.

In reviewing the market from around 2000, as a baseline, we can observe a dichotomy between market segments. The apparent conflicts between the taxi and TNC are in part a result of successful attempts, on the part of TNCs, to establish an app-specific market share. Larger TNCs appear adept in arguing their case as technology companies, rather than transport companies per se, despite the effective banality of the argument, with taxis and TNCs doing effectively the same thing, often with the same or similar technologies. Indeed, on the basis of the TNC argument, it is possible to conclude that taxi companies are technology platforms, accepting bookings and dispatching vehicles. The retention of an exclusive hailing function, by taxis in many cities, may prove to be a poisoned chalice, rather than the effective distinguisher it had been promised to be.

New entrant TNCs, in distinguishing their operation without the weight of regulatory burdens applied to the taxi industry, have been able to challenge the traditional regulated competition in the market and instead establish a closure to free-market approach to competition.

The TNC market was further enhanced by the large-scale introduction of vehicle operations using non-professional drivers. The market for non-professional supply eclipsed earlier use of an existing licensed professional driver; and based, in no small part, on the argument of regulatory ambiguities, the larger TNCs were able to apply their lobbying power to create favourable regulatory environments on a large scale, as opposed to the traditional taxi industry focusing on local markets. The argument highlighted, even created, market ambiguities that despite myriad visits to litigation, in and out of court, remained persistently favoured by the public as effective, cheap, and reliable. If ambiguity had not been present prior to the TNC white paper, it certainly did thereafter.

Changing Economic Properties

The most recent technological innovations, most based on the use of an app, can present a series of potential solutions to the, recurring, economic issues of the taxi mode. These related to a series of market issues including, but not limited to: information symmetry; market equilibria, between supply and demand; employment status, rights, and costs; industry pricing, including market and monopolistic pricing; and operational optimisation.

The ability, of the app, to display full trip fare, prior to its commencement, has the ability to significantly enhance the amount of information available to the, intending, passenger. Traditionally, arguments are made that an intending passenger has little or no access to fare information prior to the start of the journey. It can equally be argued that a passenger may be unaware, in reality, of the likely actual fare until the end of the journey. In both instances, the passenger has little or no ability to compare fares between suppliers, the passenger needing to make a value judgement on the cost and fairness of the amount being charged, while facing a significant disutility penalty of not taking the first taxi regardless of their perception of the driver's honesty; effectively a market failure on multiple fronts. In the traditional taxi market, these elements have led to the adoption of a regulated price, being set, typically as a maximum, by the regulator and imposed on the trade. Despite multiple issues, complaints, and court cases, the practice remains commonly applied in most cities and would typically result in a tariff review being undertaken on a defined interval basis.

The digitisation of the booking process provides a new opportunity for fare display and information on fare calculation. TNCs are frequently permitted to display an 'upfront' fare based around, but exactly upon, the same principles of time and distance visible in the traditional industry. The statement of a known and unchangeable fare up front has been widely popular amongst passengers, where the amount is defined and known comparisons are, at least in theory, far more possible. The drawback being few of the traditional suppliers are able, or willing, to adopt the same practice. This leaves the upfront fare relatively uncontested and potentially creates the circumstances for profit maximising behaviours, even monopolistic abuse. This said, the presence of the upfront fare does score highly amongst reported analysis and is likely to remain popular where perceived to be based on a reasoned calculation and comparing reasonably with other vehicle types for the same trip.

Digitisation further enhances other areas where information asymmetry had previously been common. The technology has allowed the near-instant third-party mutual verification of driver and passenger, and the allied practice of driver and passenger ratings. While both drivers and passengers retain the ability, and right, to select each other on their mutual view, of each other, the development of independent scoring systems maintained on the respective TNC apps allows both the driver and passenger to engage in a beauty contest, selecting only reputable drivers or choosing to accept bookings from passengers without negative histories.

Similarly, the organisational form allowed by digitisation, by using platforms where the TNC acts as an intermediary, addresses the recurring problem of excess or insufficient supply at the fleet level. The basic imbalances can be partially addressed by increasing the use of part-time workers and vehicles in a fleet. This step, however, has resulted in a range of new issues relating to the legal status of the workers and liabilities and is felt to have only partial success in resolving the issue of dis-equilibria from the supply side. Legal challenge aside, though these remain highly important in and of themselves, a further practice rested to peak price penalties, sometimes called surge pricing, seeks to influence demand (downward) by increasing cost of use at points of highest supply. The increased cost reflected in higher incomes and thus, it is argued, resulting in higher levels of supply. The argument works best where actual fluctuations in price, which had included multiples, including significant multiples, of base fare, are known. The actual extent of fare increases in response to demand being more recently hidden by the adoption of upfront statements of fare.

From the consumer side, the main effect of the technological developments has so far been to make the industry relatively more attractive compared to other modes. Much of this has been through a combination of offering better service and thereby reducing the barriers towards use. But an important point has been the offer of subsidised services in order to gain market shares. As the funds available for such subsidies decrease, the cost of the services will increase for the consumer and the revenue will decrease for the drivers. Both developments will probably result in decreased use. Either reducing the total number of trips, compared with today, or reducing the modal share of app-based services. The latter, despite being reported by a number of experts, seems an unlikely as these services offer some qualitative improvements over the alternatives.

Recurring and Shifting Regulations

Throughout the history of the taxi mode, the impacts and status of its regulation have been significant. Regulations have developed, and changed, to reflect the external circumstances of the mode, its supply, and the societies that use it.

The period of the 1920s, commonly allied to the Great Depression, saw the taxi mode as having 'easy entry'. Barriers to entry were relatively low, with the advent of mass-produced vehicles decreasing the cost of entry further. High levels of unemployment, a result of the depression, were contracted to the taxi market's potential as a job, albeit an employment of last resort for some. The mass entry to the trade, cutthroat, and destructive competition led to a backlash against lenient regulation, and the rapid imposition of struct controls, seen, at the time, as necessary to protect the public interest.

Regulatory direction shifted visibly in the 1980s, with the adoption of deregulation across both the US and European markets. The moves reflected wider neo-liberal principles of privatisation and liberalisation. While many of these affected the taxi industry, only some remain, as the harsh and widespread deregulations in the US were followed by a retrenchment and re-regulation.

The current regulatory changes, from the early 2010s, combine elements of both ideology, economic rationale, and a shift in the fundamental economics of the business. Ideology, as the deregulator sentiment, for removing barriers to entry and for challenging established industries remains. Economic rationales can also be identified, with few reasons within economics to maintain entry barriers and strong regulation on industries with voluntary supply and demand, as long as the negative externalities for society are limited. The industry is also facing a shift in its underlying economics, as booking can be automated and removed from the geographic scale of physical service provision. It remains to be seen if this round of changing regulation will result in a new round of the regulatory cycle or establish a new and radically different market than what was in place in 2010. Irrespective of outcome, the current developments present both winners and losers.

Actor Perspectives

Of the main winners and losers, of the current round of reform, established taxi owners can be suggested to have suffered the most, especially in jurisdictions where the number of taxis has historically been strictly controlled.

Locations with high historic medallion values have also experienced substantial market changes, where the taxi licences or medallion have been an openly tradable commodity, and in some instances, where its transfer value is less obvious and/or hidden. The greatest loss of confidence/licence value occurs where new market entrants are subject to fewer controls, in general, and no number or licence caps in particular. Revenue streams previously accruing to licence holder, and to the subsidiary medallion financing industry, have suddenly become a lot lower. The market shock is significant to the underlying economics of particular cities, with New York often cited. Key also is the relationships between the city authorities and the value gains (losses) associated with medallion purchase.

The various difficulties of the traditional industry reflect the relative incompatibility of the two market forms, open and regulated competition.

For the driver community, the historical changes have not all been negative. TNC drivers benefitted from the emergence of a new sector, with associated employment opportunities. An increase in the FHV market share may also have had a positive benefit on individual drivers, while reverse benefits have arisen from the departure and retirement of drivers, allowing those remaining to pick up a greater number of trips. The latter growth is of particular significance over the pandemic. TNC technologies, and those of some taxi companies, have also benefitted the driver community, particularly in the introduction of ancillary transport services. Larger TNCs appear particularly adept in the development of additional market segments away from traditional passenger transportation, including food delivery, grocery and small freight, and a range of further specialist transport services. The advent of non-passenger transport was not unknown to the traditional taxi industry but has been significantly increased, particularly in the field of fast-food delivery, as app companies have invested in the development of restaurant delivery platforms, adjacent to their passenger offering, and making use of downtime within the fleet.

In the most recent time period, and ongoing at the time of writing, a scarcity of labour has emerged as an issue. In some countries, including Norway, this has led to a de facto increase in wages, sometimes associated with higher mileage rates, particularly amongst TNCs, while in other markets, the increase follows from a higher number of trips allocated across a smaller number of drivers. For the operators of vehicle owners, the long-term effect might be allied to reduction of profitability, where total market share is lost to new entrants, with the possible further impact of delayed updates to vehicles within the fleet – a reduction in the quality of the vehicles used. The effects appear also to have been speeded up by the Covid pandemic but has had various and in part contradictory effects in the long term.

Labour relations and availability have also emerged as a theme across many jurisdictions. The ongoing dispute whether drivers qualify as employees or as self-employed independent contractors appears unresolved globally, though a weight of evidence has been established with court decisions and precedent suggesting a right for drivers to be considered employees, and thus entitled to statutory worker rights, including health care and retirement schemes in some instances. This said, regulations are also in flux, or at least the scale of regulation, that is being directly affected by the spatial definition of an authority area and the potential for significant differences in scale of regulatory authority between taxi and TNC. Not all locations interpret national or federal legislation in the same way, while some including cities in California have allowed ballots to decide specific rights, with the result, in some locations, that significant campaigning has been seen.

TNCs have also spent much of their existence arguing strongly that they represent a separate, and unique, section of the FHV market, separate from and deserving of different treatment compared to the legacy industry. The argument has generally prevailed, with many authorities, particularly those in North America, choosing to adopt a separate regulation for the new entrant. This said, the passage of time has seen many such services becoming increasingly integrated into the FHV industry, in many locations, and into the wider public transport industry in some. Differences between TNCs and traditional operators have been focused on organisational structure as status as technology companies, particularly by the TNCs themselves. The passage of time reduced actual differences as the legacy industry moved slowly towards the same technologies, while aspects of the traditional industry that had once made it unique within the FHV industry, namely the provision of physical mobility services, education transport, and similar, have also been taken up by the TNC segment, reducing and/or eliminating all but the most limited differential, namely the right to pick up on street. As the two sides of the industry continue to converge, even this 'right' may disappear: its loss may actually further assist the industry develop.

Future Outlooks

Any attempt at future prediction is, and has been demonstrated, to be partial at best. The taxi industry is as good an example of this as any, but clear patterns can and have been demonstrated. Changes in technologies will, almost inevitably, lead to a step change in the industries those changes impact. Some will welcome such changes, some will oppose them, often with vehement argument, almost mirroring the stages of grief of any loss.

It is equally clear that the current FHV market is not in a steady state. The loss of equilibrium presented by the initial launch of the (new) TNC technologies has changed the nature of the industry, forever. New equilibrium appears to have come and gone, with each substantive change to the app technology and/or its application further disturbing the balance between suppliers. Launches of restaurant delivery, accessibility, and transit functions within the TNC platform create a new balance at each occurrence, with a likelihood that these will not be the last such change.

Trends, in terms of technology, economics, demographics, and culture, will continue to influence the FHV markets in the future. The market for the services that are provided by the FHV actors is likely to increase in size and relevance as part of the total mobility services. However, the industry will likely continue to change, not only in response to the overall trends and technologies available but also as a result of shifting cultures for its use, the role it is envisioned in the larger mobility market and market interventions.

Immediate changes are most likely to follow the demand for service supply, with previously unthinkable linkages between TNC and taxi fleets continuing for as long as mutual benefit remains. Taxi companies may, eventually, catch up on the quality and complexity of the TNC platforms, join them, or simply emulate them by becoming TNCs themselves. Significant also is the potential move from two-tiered licensing systems to single tiers, and with it multiple revisits to the question whether to regulate, what to regulate, and by whom. Visible arguments maintain the right of the public to expect safe services, with oversight. Protecting the public interest, a key tenet of the very earlier regulations, has not gone away. Neither can regulations, at least not those that continue to serve the base purpose.

Glossary

Applications (smartphone apps)	Apps	A computer program designed specifically for operation on a smartphone.
Closed markets		Constrained markets/capped markets that prevent the entry of new participants, including by the use of regulated maxima applied to the number of participants, licences that may be issued, including by the application of licence constraints.
Cut-throat competition		A variation on the concept of destructive competition, though potentially considered to have less harm, where an excess number of suppliers adopt undesirable business practices to secure market share. Often created where the number of FHVs exceeds the public demand for them, resulting in drivers and/or companies breaking rules against over-charging and short trip service refusals, and cutting corners on vehicle maintenance, insurance, and related operating costs.
Demand responsive transport (*US Eng: Transportation*)	DRT	Any form of passenger transport available on demand, at the request of an intending passenger at or near to the time of (desired) use. The term typically refers to public transport services that include an on-demand component, either by being a scheduled service only being driven when there is a stated demand or being a semi-scheduled service offering almost door-to-door service.
Deregulation		Literally the removal of (some elements of) regulation. Frequently related to the removal of licence caps (derestriction). May also include the removal of (some) limits applied to company type and operating procedures (liberalisation).

(Continued)

Farebox		Literally, a box into which a fare is deposited. Used as a conceptual description of (all) fares received for the provision of transport, whether tendered in cash or by other means.
For hire vehicle	FHV	Taxis, PHV/private hire, and TNCs. May also include jitneys, taxibuses, and other vehicle types available on demand, with driver, for remuneration. Often used interchangeably with the term vehicle for hire.
Free market competition		An open market that supports a competitive equilibrium as a result of producer and consumer responses. In reality, all (legal) markets fall into the continuum between regulated and free market competition and all will be subject to some form of regulation.
Gig economy		A relatively informal or flexible sector of the economy related to the nature of employment and flexibility of accepting work. A gig worker may enter into a contract to provide a service(s) (to work a gig) on demand at the choice of the worker. Gig work can include elements under the control of an 'employer', who may define prices/rates, and the allocation of tasks, and can include distribution platforms and automated task allocation algorithms.
Hard to serve area		A description of areas which have demonstrably lower levels of supply. May relate to a physical, geographical, area which is typically avoided by drivers or particular populations. Some references to the areas include 'wrong side of the river/bridge/tracks'. The lack of service may be caused by (perceived) lack of trade as affecting driver choice.
Industrial price index	IPI	A measure of the costs of service provision as specific to the industry. Sometimes, used as a synonym for taxi cost index, particularly where related to the measurement and increase in taxi fares.
Information communications and technologies	ICT	Any technology that supports the communication of data, typically using digital transmission. The term can be used in differing ways and applied to a wide range of digital technologies, including both software and hardware.
Jitney		A form of taxi transport for the carriage of multiple passengers travelling at separate fares. Can be based on a line service that follows a defined route, or an area of service that will define origin and destination to the needs of the passenger's precise request. Can be used as a synonym for taxibus.

Level playing field		The concept that different market participants operate under the same set of regulations or controls. A market does not need to be uncontrolled to be 'level' but rather all participants operate under the same set of controls and thus have an equal opportunity to compete (market equality/parity of opportunity).
Livery		Originating from a formal uniform or identity, the term has entered use in FHV supply as related to a standardised vehicle appearance. Some fleets, particularly in the limousine and private hire sectors, may also be referred to as livery vehicles. In some US cities, the term is used in place of 'black car' or a similar term as a form of service category.
Market failure		The concept that an open and free market may fail to deliver beneficial competitive outcomes. Examples in the provision of FHV services include 'instant monopolies' created by a lack of alternatives for street hail, or as a result of 'first screen preference' for app bookings, and providing a justification, in the case of the taxi market, for fare controls.
Mobility as a service	MaaS	Conceptual definition of all forms of transport as may be used, singularly or in combination, to provide transport from any origin to any destination. To include, but not be limited to, any aspect of provision that supports delivery, including information provision, booking, ticketing, and feedback. Maas is a term used with different meanings by different actors. In Europe and Australia, it mainly refers to the integration of a public transport-centred service with a common user interface.
Non-emergency medical transport	NEMT	Transport service provided for the use of passengers accessing or returning from medical treatment that does not qualify as urgent or life-threatening (emergency).
Paradigm shift		A fundamental and, generally, irreversible alteration in the market.
Paratransit		A term related to the concept of equal access, particularly in relation to the Americans with Disabilities Act, where it originates from the concept of providing specialist vehicle types in parallel to existing transit services (mainly public transport bus services).
Passenger service vehicle	PSV	Any vehicle intended to carry passengers, usually for commercial use, with passengers paying a fare. Most frequently applied to bus services.
Present value	PV	Can also be expressed as a net present value (NPV) being a measurement of benefits net of costs.

(Continued)

Private hire vehicle	PHV	A form of FHV available on request by pre-booking, not able to ply-for-hire nor pick up at taxi stands. Other terms include private hire car (PHC) – Scotland; private hire taxi – Northern Ireland; and 'Hackney' – Republic of Ireland.
Professional/non-professional drivers		Distinction based on the extent to which a driver is regulated and/or required to work defined hours or at defined times of day, day of week, etc. The definition is important when distinguishing between the working practices of taxi drivers and more flexible working practices in the TNC sector/gig economy.
Public transport		(US/Canada: Transit). Any form of mass transportation providing commercial planned transportation, typically on a line basis, using defined stopping points.
Quantity, quality, and economic controls	QQE	The regulatory domains within which a significant majority of taxi regulations are defined.
Regulated competition		A form of market competition that includes intervention(s) on some aspects of market operation, typically by a regulator or regulatory agency.
Return on investment	ROI	The amount of measurable benefit that may arise from an individual investment. Would typically be expressed as a ratio using valuation of both costs and (monetary) return. Can also be expressed as a social return on investment (SROI) where social benefits are included as a monetised return.
Street taxi		A taxi that is operated exclusively to the street hail and stand markets. A street taxi will not typically be equipped to accept dispatched trips.
Transportation network company	TNC	An FHV company providing vehicles for hire with driver on a commercial basis on the basis of bookings made on or via an on-line platform, typically an app. Can also be referred to as a private transportation company (PTC) (Toronto), transportation network providers (TNP) (Chicago), and a variety of other terms, including ridesourcing and rideshare.
Vehicle for hire	VFH	Synonym of for hire vehicle.
Wheelchair accessible vehicle/taxi	WAV/WAT	A vehicle specifically designed for the carriage of a wheelchair with user, without the need for the user to dismount, nor the wheelchair be folded. WAVs can be purpose-built or modifications of existing vehicles, most frequently small van conversions. Can also be called a wheelchair accessible taxi (WAT) where applied to the taxi trade alone.

Index

Printed in the United States
by Baker & Taylor Publisher Services